Finding Shelter

MODULE C

Finding Shelter

Where do you go when the rain falls and the wind blows? If you know what's good for you, you head for shelter. Animals of all kinds protect themselves by building or finding shelters. Your home is a shelter, and so are the nests of birds and the dens of bears. In this module, you'll find out how different animals build shelters.

CHAPTER

1 Shelters

Where do shelters come from?
People and other animals build shelters from resources found in nature.

CHAPTER

2 Heat on the Move

Brrr! It's time to turn on the heat. Well-insulated houses keep heat on the inside and cold on the outside. They also save fuels.

CHAPTER 3 Machines in Building

Beavers bite and build. Both beavers and people use machines to build shelters. But the beavers' machines are parts of their bodies.

In this module

At the end of the book

Shelters

How can you build a shelter?

Imagine that your family is taking a hike in a forest and gets lost. It is getting late. You are going to have to spend the night in the forest. You need a shelter of some kind. Make a model of the kind of shelter you might build.

For Discussion

1. *Why do you need a shelter?*

2. *What could you use to build your shelter?*

1.1 Resources in Shelters

Why do people need shelters?

In the early morning, this family watched storm clouds gather overhead and listened to the low rumble of thunder. Now, rain soaks their clothing and turns their cereal and toast into a mushy mess.

Would you like to join the family in the picture for breakfast? Your answer most likely is, "No way!" When rain comes or when snowflakes fall, what do you do? You probably head for a **shelter**—something that covers and protects.

From early times, people have built shelters to protect themselves from the weather and from danger. In this lesson, you will find out what materials people use to build shelters.

◄ This family could use a shelter to keep the rain off themselves and their food. Even the dog is under the table out of the rain!

➤ *Lumber is often used to build the framework of a house.*

Building Shelters

Remember what you decided you might use to build your shelter in the Discover Activity? Was it the materials you could find in the forest? For hundreds of years, people have built shelters of materials they can get easily. Some people still use materials found near where they live, but many people use materials that are produced far away.

What material was used to build the framework for a house in the picture? Yes, it's lumber. But do you know how lumber is made? Let's find out.

From Forest to Lumberyard

Trees are cut down, branches are trimmed off, and logs are loaded onto trucks.

Trucks haul the logs to a lumber mill to be cut into different sizes and made smooth.

Lumber is made from wood, and wood comes from trees. Like clay, stone, and many other materials people use to build shelters, trees are a natural resource. A **natural resource** is a material that comes from the earth and can be used by living things. Most of the trees now used to make lumber grow in the southeastern United States and along the Pacific coast of North America. However, trees, like many natural resources, usually are not used as they are found in nature.

Look at the pictures that show the steps between cutting down trees and lumber arriving at the lumberyard. Over the years, many changes have taken place in the way lumber is made. More and better machines are being built to produce lumber.

Of course, lumber is only one of the materials you need for a house. Imagine having a house without windows or a foundation to hold it up! So you need glass and concrete. Also, you may want to use brick for the outside walls.

Trucks haul finished lumber to a lumberyard to be sold.

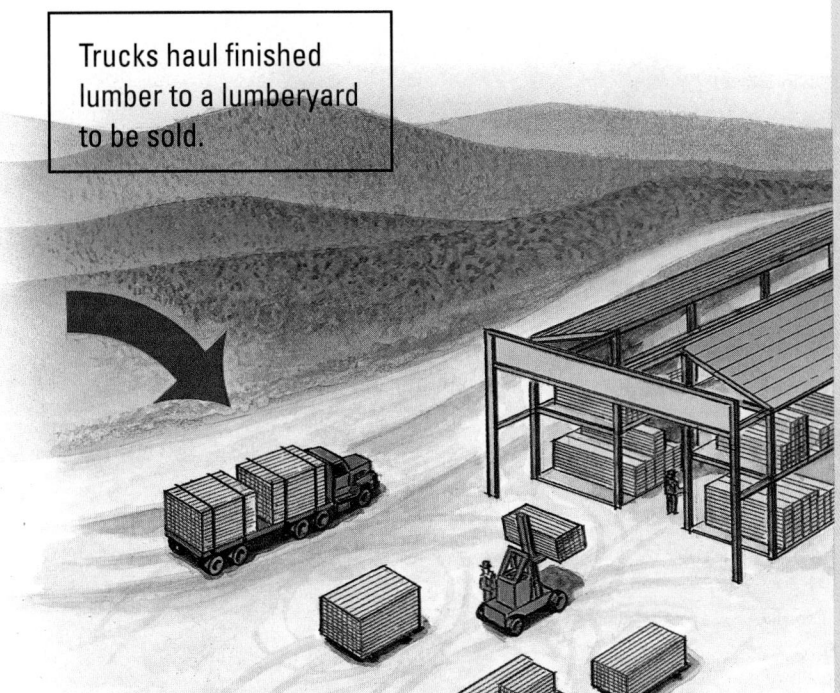

Which Is Softer?

How can you find out how soft wood is without pounding a nail into it? Let's investigate.

What To Do
A. Fill a metal pan or dish with water.
B. Place a 3-centimeter cube of balsa and of pine in water.

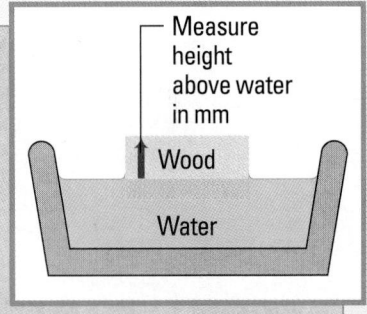

Measure height above water in mm
Wood
Water

C. Measure the height in millimeters that each cube sticks above the water. Record it in a chart such as the one shown below.

Record Your Results

Wood	Height Out of Water
Balsa	
Pine	

What Did You Find Out?
1. *The higher the wood floats in water, the softer it is. Which wood is softer?*
2. *Which wood would be better for building a house? Why?*

Sources of Building Materials

Natural resources are the beginning of many materials.

Look around! The chair that you sit on and the pen you're holding are made from natural resources. What materials from the earth went into these objects? Find other things in your classroom—the chalkboard and chalk perhaps—and name the natural resources used to make them.

The building materials in homes and schools often are made from natural resources. For example, the bricks and glass in a building are made from natural resources.

How Glass Is Made

Step 1: A large amount of sand is heated with small amounts of lime (from limestone) and soda (from salt or another mineral).

Step 2: The mixture is then cooled and shaped into glass.

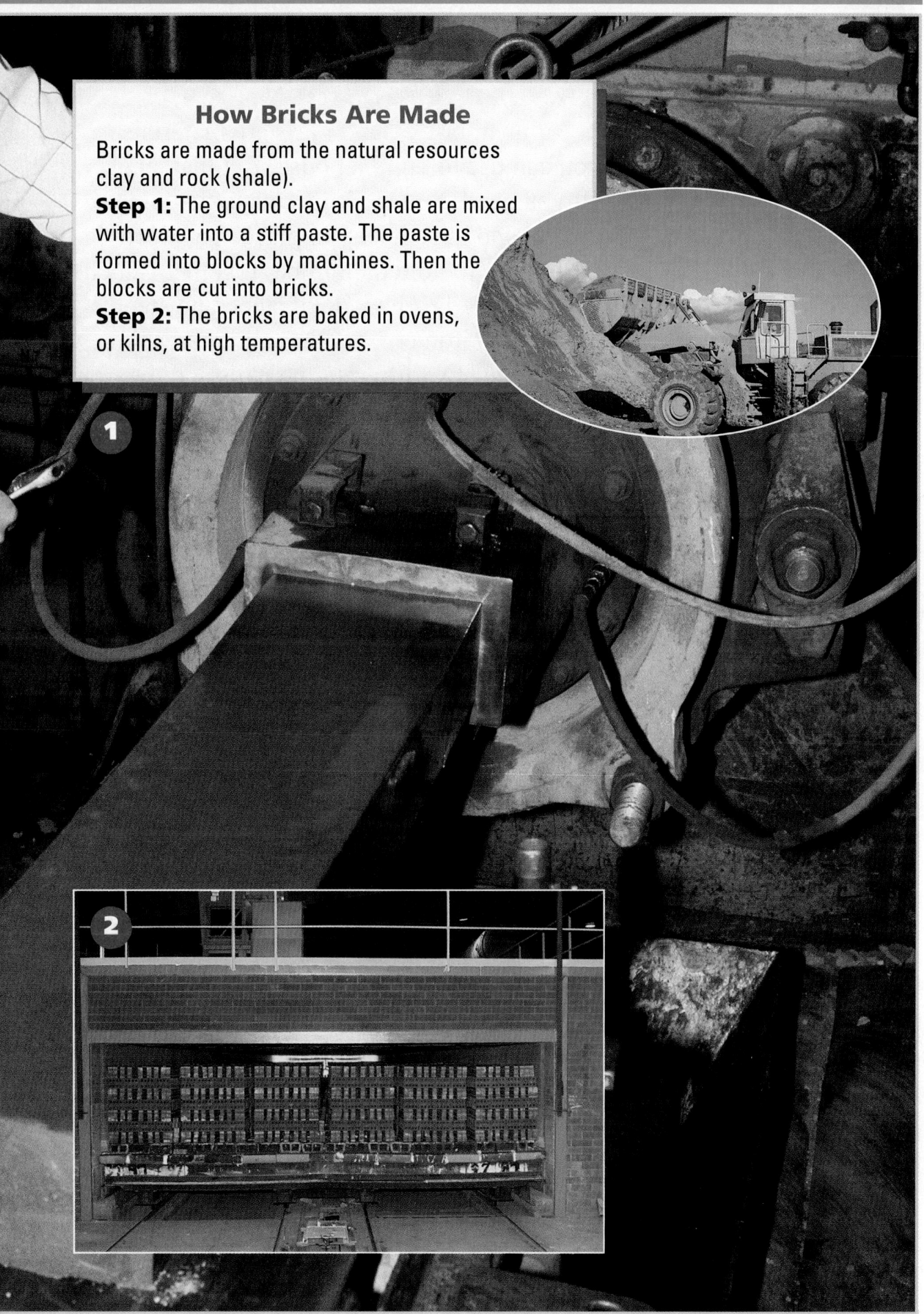

How Bricks Are Made

Bricks are made from the natural resources clay and rock (shale).

Step 1: The ground clay and shale are mixed with water into a stiff paste. The paste is formed into blocks by machines. Then the blocks are cut into bricks.

Step 2: The bricks are baked in ovens, or kilns, at high temperatures.

Keeping It Together

Lumber, bricks, and glass are materials you can use to build a house. But that's not all you need. You can't just stand the lumber on end and have it stay in place. You need something to hold the lumber together—such as a nail. Nails are made of steel, and steel is made from iron ore, another natural resource. But notice how different the nails and the iron ore in the pictures look. Let's find out how to get steel nails from iron ore.

The open-pit mine in the picture is huge. Miners use power shovels to scoop up the ore from the pits. Trucks, ships, and railroads carry the ore to steel plants. At the steel plant, iron is separated from the ore in huge furnaces—higher than a ten-story building! The melted iron collects in a pool at the bottom of the furnace.

Remember that nails are made from steel, not iron. So, how is iron made into steel? Melted iron is heated to a very high temperature with a small amount of carbon. The melted iron and carbon combine to form liquid steel, which is poured into molds. The liquid steel hardens in the molds. Giant rollers squeeze the steel into long narrow strips of wire.

▼ Steel nails are made from iron ore, which comes from iron mines such as this open-pit mine in Minnesota.

At a nail factory, machines cut the wire and shape the point of the nail at one end. At the same time, the machine hammers the other end of the nail to make the head. One machine can make over 500 nails in a minute!

Now, if the outside walls of the house are bricks, nails won't help. To hold bricks together, you need cement—made of two natural resources, limestone and clay. Limestone comes from a gravel pit such as the one in the picture. Dry cement, shown in the picture, is mixed with water and sand to make a thick paste, or mortar. The mortar, shown on a trowel in the picture, is then placed between bricks with a trowel. When the mortar hardens, it will keep those bricks in place for years!

▲ Limestone comes from a gravel pit and is used to make cement. A trowel is used to put mortar between bricks.

Checkpoint

1. Where do natural resources come from?
2. What natural resources are used to make bricks and glass?
3. What natural resources are used to hold building materials together?
4. **Take Action!** Look around one room of your house and list all the building materials that come from natural resources.

Observing Different Building Materials

Building materials differ in many ways. Observe some materials to find out how they are different.

Picture A

Gather These Materials

brick	pebbles
burlap	rock
concrete	sticks
leaves	thick, clear plastic
mud	wood

Picture B

Picture C

Follow This Procedure

1 Make a chart like the one on the next page. Record your results on your chart.

2 Look closely at the building materials that are displayed on the table. (Picture A) What do you think these materials might be used for?

3 Pick up one of the materials. What do you think it is? Observe how it feels—rough or smooth, what it looks like, how big it is, and how heavy it is. (Picture B)

Predict: *If the pieces were the same size, which materials would be heaviest?*

4 Record your observations of the building material.

5 Repeat steps 3 and 4 for each of the other materials. (Picture C)

State Your Conclusions

1. Which material feels rough? smooth?

2. Imagine you have equal-sized pieces of each material. Which material do you think would be lightest? heaviest?

3. Think about what you have learned about natural resources. What natural resource might each of these materials be made from?

Let's Experiment

From your observations of these materials, which of them do you think would be best to use for the roof of a shelter if you lived where there was a lot of rain? Use what you know about scientific methods to find out.

Record Your Results

Material	Description	Use

Into The Field

What kinds of shelters do animals use?

Observe animal shelters in your neighborhood. Draw or describe each shelter.

➤ A gray squirrel has built a nest in a hollow tree to shelter its babies in the picture on the next page.

LESSON

1.2 *Using Resources Found Nearby*

▶ **What natural resources do animals use for shelters?**

A small gray squirrel sits at the base of an oak tree eating an acorn. Every few seconds its head turns from side to side, its beady eyes on the lookout for danger. Suddenly, the wind starts to blow and it begins to snow hard! What happens next? The squirrel races up the tree and dives into its nest.

Animal Shelters

Like people, animals need shelter. They need protection from the rain, snow, heat, cold, and from other animals. They need a safe place in which to raise their young. Many animals find shelter in hollow trees, under logs, or in other places. Other animals build their own shelters or add natural resources to the shelters they find.

Now, from the squirrel's point of view, the ideal nest is a hole high up in a large tree or in a hollow tree trunk. Finding a hole means less work for the squirrel. It has only to clean out any rotten wood and make a nest. For the nest, the squirrel might use grass, leaves, pieces of bark, and twigs. A nest, such as the one in the picture, keeps the baby squirrels safe, dry, and warm.

Like squirrels, beavers use trees—that great natural resource—to build shelters. They build lodges at the shore or in the middle of a pond or river. The dome of the lodge will rise from a meter to twelve meters above the water line. Notice what the beaver lodge in the picture looks like.

How do beavers build such a huge lodge? It's really quite simple—if you're a beaver. Notice in the picture how the beaver uses its strong front teeth to cut down trees. Beavers also use their teeth to peel the bark and branches off the trees.

A beaver then holds a branch, or even a log, tightly between its teeth. With the branch in its mouth the beaver swims back to the place it has chosen for its lodge. The beavers pile up the branches and weave them together to make a lodge.

▼ *Beavers need to be good "lumberjacks" to cut down enough trees to build their lodges.*

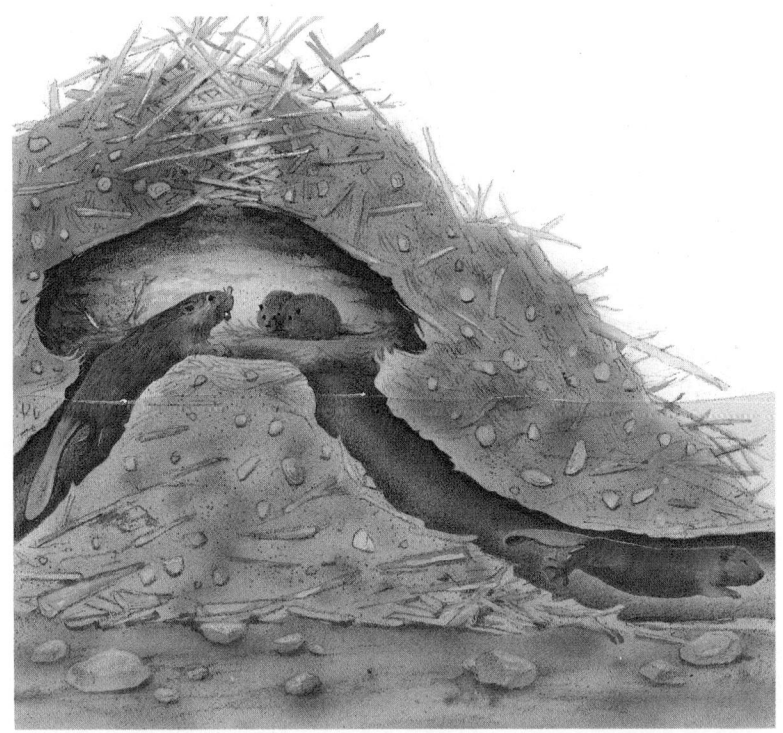

◄ *The entrances to the tunnels leading to the beavers' lodge are underwater.*

▲ *A beaver carries a branch in its mouth and swims back to the lodge it is building.*

Using their teeth, the beavers tunnel up from the bottom of the pond. They gnaw through the bottom of the lodge and hollow out a den. Find the two tunnels leading to the lodge in the picture. Beavers use these tunnels to get in and out of the lodge.

While the lodge is quite comfortable in warm weather, the loose tangle of sticks and branches wouldn't keep out cold winter winds. So before ice forms on the pond, the beavers plaster the outside of the lodge. A beaver uses its paws to scoop up rotted leaves and mud from the bottom of the pond. Then the beaver pats and punches the wet material into spaces between the sticks. It leaves a small opening at the top of the lodge to let in air. When the weather gets cold, the mud freezes solid. Like the squirrels in their nest, the beavers will be safe and warm.

This log cabin is typical of those built in America by early European settlers.

In 1892, many people in Nebraska lived in houses made of sod blocks.

Shelters in Early America

Native Americans who settled in the woodlands of North America made houses of wood covered with bark. Later, European settlers also built their homes of wood. Look at the picture of the log cabin. The settlers filled the spaces between the logs with mud and moss. As settlers moved westward, they found many kinds of shelters built by Native Americans. Each tribe of people made houses with materials they could find easily.

On the Great Plains, only a few trees grew along the riverbanks. Native Americans who lived there built earth lodges made of logs thickly covered with hard-packed grass and dirt. The settlers, who had plows and spades, cut sod into blocks, such as those shown in the picture. They piled the blocks one on top of the other to form the walls of the house. Notice in the picture that the roof of the house was also made of logs and sod.

In the Southwest, Native Americans built homes with the resources they had nearby—stone and mud. They built flat-roofed rooms and placed them side by side and on top of one another. The buildings looked somewhat like apartment houses of today.

◄ These Mexican women are building a house of adobe brick. Finished houses often looked like the one shown below.

In lowland parts of the Southwest, Native Americans made houses of adobe—a mixture of sandy clay, water, and straw. They shaped the mixture into lumps. When the lumps hardened, the people used the same mixture to plaster lumps together into thick walls. The walls kept out both heat and cold.

Later, people who moved up from Mexico also made their homes of adobe. But they shaped the adobe into bricks. Notice the bricks and the adobe houses in the pictures. Before long, Native Americans were also making their houses out of bricks. Even today, the kind of shelters that people build depends on where they live and what material they can get easily.

Checkpoint

1. How are the shelters of squirrels and beavers alike?
2. Why didn't all Native Americans use the same building materials?
3. **Take Action!** Make a thick paste with flour and water, and put it on waxed paper to dry. How would you describe the dried paste?

Activity

Building a Bird's Nest

Think about a bird's nest or pictures of nests you have seen. Then try to build a bird's nest.

Picture A

Picture B

Picture C

Gather These Materials

shirt-box lid   string
small twigs   mud
straw   water
long, dry grass

Follow This Procedure

1 Make a chart like the one on the next page. Record your results on your chart.

2 Use the box lid to build the nest in.

3 Take a few handfuls of twigs and straw and place them in the box lid. (Picture A) Count how many handfuls of each material you use. Record how much of each material you use.

4 Arrange the materials in a circle, and build up the edges of the circle—leaving a hollow in the center.

5 Use the grass and string to twist and weave around the twigs and straw to hold them together. (Picture B)

6 Cover the circle of dry materials with mud. Pat and pinch the muddy materials into a bowllike shape. (Picture C)

7 Add drops of water to the mud if needed to keep the mud damp while you shape the nest.

> **Predict: *What will happen to the nest when the mud dries?***

8 Keep on shaping the nest as the mud begins to dry so the nest will keep its bowllike shape and be large enough to hold three or four small bird's eggs.

State Your Conclusions

1. What was difficult about building the bird's nest?

2. Think about what you know about building materials. What other materials might also be used to make a nest?

Let's Experiment

Now that you have built a bird's nest, how do you think birds get their nests to stay where they build them? Without climbing a tree, use what you know about scientific methods to find out.

Record Your Results

Material	How much used

Making Inferences

Suppose you go outside. It is sunny, but there are puddles all over. Would you think that it had recently rained? You have made an inference, or a guess based on what you observe and what you already know. You know that rain is one cause of puddles.

Scientists cannot always answer all their questions just by examining something. So they combine data they observe with what they already know. This step helps them infer likely answers to their questions.

Thinking It Through

You know that many animals build shelters. These homes shelter them from rain and cold or protect their babies. Suppose you see a nest high in a tree. What can you infer about the animal that uses it? You might use these questions to help you.

1. What can I observe?
I can see that it is a nest and that it is high up in a tree.
2. What do I already know from other situations?
I know an animal that uses a nest for a shelter must have built this shelter. I also know that an animal that builds its nest in a high place must be able to climb or fly to reach it.
3. Can I make an inference from these two kinds of facts?
The animal that built this shelter is one that builds a nest, and it can either fly or climb trees. It is most likely a squirrel or a bird.

You see an animal shelter that is half underwater and half out of the water in a deep lake. It is made of branches that have been chewed off of trees and dragged from the land into the water. Is this shelter most likely the home of a water bird, a fish, a mammal that can swim, an insect, or a snake? Support your inference with specific details.

Chapter Review

Thinking Back

1. Explain why people build **shelters.**
2. What **natural resources** are used to make glass?
3. How are nails made?
4. How are animal shelters like those that people build?
5. What materials did Native Americans and early European settlers use for shelters? Why?

Connecting Ideas

1. Copy the concept map. Use the terms at the right to complete the map about resources for building.

shelters   bricks   lumber   iron ore   limestone

Natural Resources   **Building Materials**

- A. trees — E. _____
- B. clay — F. _____
- C. _____ — G. steel
- D. _____ — H. cement
- I. _____

2. Write a sentence or two about the ideas in the concept map.

Gathering Evidence

1. In the Activity on page 12, what scientific methods did you use to compare materials?
2. In the Activity on page 20, how did you know that mud is helpful in building a nest?

Doing Science!

1. **Build** a miniature log cabin, sod house, or adobe shelter.
2. **Make a list** of what natural resources are available in your area to build shelters for people and shelters for animals.

Heat on the Move

Oh wow, that's weird!

What makes things feel warm?

Put ice water in one bowl, room-temperature water in a second bowl, and warm water in a third. Place one hand in the ice water and one in the warm water for 1 minute. Describe how each hand feels. Then put both hands in the room-temperature water. Now how do your hands feel?

For Discussion

1. Why did your hands feel differently?

2. How do you explain your observations?

2.1 *Heat in Shelters*

How do shelters help animals?

Outside, an icy wind howls and the temperature drops below zero, but Snoopy doesn't care! Notice in the picture that Snoopy has space heaters to keep him warm. In real life, however, animals don't have heaters! People who have pets usually keep them inside, but what about other animals? How do animals in the wild keep warm? How do unheated shelters help animals stay warm?

Heating Up

You might remember the lizard absorbs energy from the sun to warm its body. The bodies of lizards don't produce their own heat. The bodies of lizards and many other animals in the world have the same temperature as their surroundings. But the bodies of other animals, such as dogs, deer, birds, and you, produce their own heat. These animals get heat from the energy in the food they eat. These animals don't have to depend on the sun to heat their bodies. The bodies of these animals are always warm and give off heat to their surroundings.

In the Discover Activity, you learned that heat always flows from warm places and objects to cooler ones. Let's see how this fact affects shelters.

PEANUTS reprinted by permission of UFS, Inc.

▲ *Of course, dogs don't really have space heaters, but some dogs might wish they did.*

Conductors and Insulators

You might think that on a cold day it wouldn't take long for an animal's body to lose all of its heat. But the animal's fur or feathers and its shelter help keep heat from moving away from the animal. How do feathers, fur, and shelters help keep animals warm?

To answer this question, you have to think about different materials. Have you ever left a metal spoon in a bowl of hot soup and then picked up the spoon? If so, you know that the spoon got hot. It got hot because the metal is a good conductor. A **conductor** is a material through which energy moves easily. The heat from the soup moved through the metal to your hand and you felt the heat.

Other materials, such as wood and plastic, are not good conductors of heat. These materials are called insulators. An **insulator** is a material through which energy does not flow easily. Another material through which heat does not flow easily is air. Air is an insulator. On cold days, animals fluff their fur or feathers to hold more air, which helps keep the animals from losing heat.

Polar bears need a shelter to protect their young.

Most birds use nests for their eggs and to raise their babies.

When building their shelters, these animals use natural resources. These natural resources are often good insulators. Squirrels, for example, line their nests with moss, dried grasses, leaves, and bark. Birds, too, line their nests with materials that are good insulators. The bird's nest in the picture is lined with feathers and milkweed seeds such as those shown in the picture.

Even snow is an insulator because the snow has a lot of air trapped in it! The polar bear in the picture digs a tunnel in the snow. Then the bear packs down the snow at the end of the tunnel to make a den. The snow helps to keep the cold air out and the bear's body heat in.

Notice the picture of the hornet's nest. The nest is made of a thin paper that the hornet makes from wood. The paper and the air in the spaces between the layers of paper are insulators. However, a hornet's nest keeps heat out—not in. Insulators help keep heat from moving—either out of or into a shelter.

▲ Hornets' nests are built to keep out heat because they only use their nests in summer.

Checkpoint

1. How do some animals produce heat in their bodies?
2. What does an insulator do?
3. **Take Action!** Make a diagram to show how conductors move heat from one object to another.

Keeping Things Warm

What kinds of materials make good insulators? Try this activity to find out how some materials compare.

Picture A

Gather These Materials

cover goggles	newspaper
3 large metal cans	3 small metal cans
dirt	warm water
leaves	3 thermometers

Follow This Procedure

1 Make a chart like the one on the next page. Record your results on your chart.

2 Put on your cover goggles.

3 Put about 3 cm of dirt into the bottom of one of the large cans. (Picture A)

4 Put the same thickness of leaves into the bottom of the second large can. The leaves should be packed down.

5 Wad some newspaper up and stuff it into the bottom of the third large can. The paper should be the same thickness as the material in the other two cans.

6 Set a small can in the center of each of the large cans. (Picture B) Surround each small can with the same material, dirt, leaves, or newspaper, that is in the bottom of the can, and pack the materials down. (Picture C)

Picture B

Picture C

Record Your Results

Can with	Water temperature		
	First	Second	Third
Dirt			
Leaves			
Newspaper			

> **Predict: *What do you think will happen to the warm water in the cans?***

7 Fill each small can with warm water, and take the temperature of the water in each can right away. Record the temperatures.

8 At the same time, take the temperature of the water in each can every 2 minutes until the temperatures change. Record the results.

State Your Conclusions

1. In which can did the temperature of the water change the fastest?

2. Using what you know about insulators, explain the changes in the temperature readings.

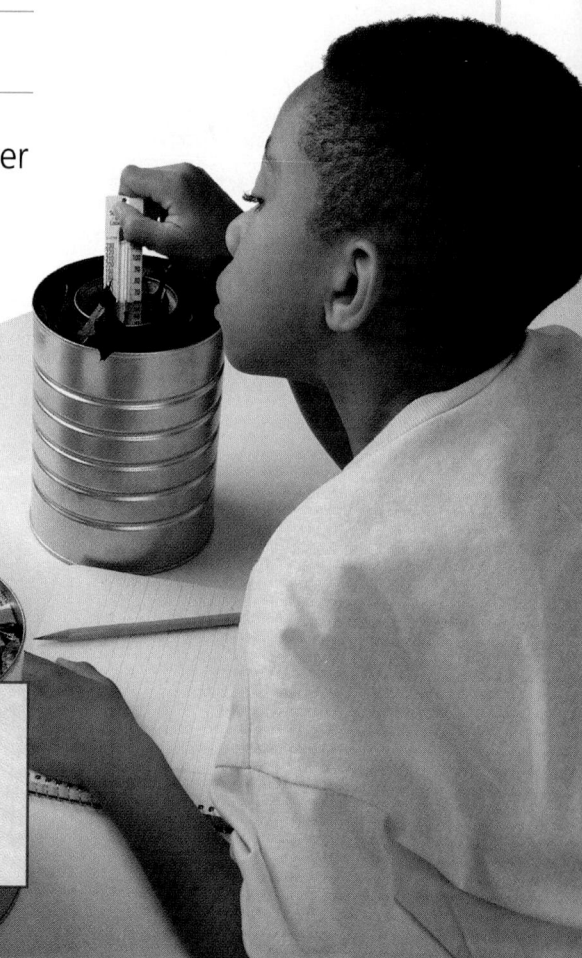

Let's Experiment

Now that you have tried wads of newspaper as an insulator, what would happen if you used finely shredded newspaper?

2.2 *Using Fuel*

► *How do people heat their homes?*

On a cold, winter day, could you warm your home with body heat the way animals do? You could if your home were the size of a fox's burrow. You might also crowd large numbers of friends and relatives into your home. But over the years, people have found ways other than body heat to warm their homes.

History of Fuel

Thousands of years ago, people discovered how to start and use a fire. Fire gave people heat, light, and a way to cook. Early people used wood to start a fire. Wood is a **fuel**—a material that can be burned to produce useful heat. Remember that wood is a natural resource that comes from trees.

▼ *Over the years, people have used different fuels to heat their shelters.*

In 1776, people burned wood for cooking and heating their homes.

Keeping the furnace filled with coal was hard work.

Wood has been used as a fuel for a longer period of time than any other fuel. In fact, it is still used as a fuel in some countries. But by the 1800s in the United States, people started looking for another source of fuel.

People began to burn coal instead of wood. Look at the pictures showing the use of different fuels in the United States. Between 1885 and 1950, coal was in wide use. But coal is dirty! And as the picture shows, people had to put the coal into the furnace or have a machine to do it for them. Also, as some of the coal supplies began to be used up, coal became more costly. People began looking for other fuels.

By the 1950s, oil and natural gas began taking the place of coal. These fuels were cleaner and were easier for people to use. Oil and gas are still the most popular fuels for heating homes today. But some people heat their homes with electricity—which, of course, is often produced by using coal.

Oil is brought to homes by trucks and stored in a large tank.

This man is reading the meter that measures how much gas is used.

Energy Sources

People use many different sources of energy to heat their homes and cook their food. They also use energy sources to run their refrigerators, toasters, and other appliances. The graph below compares the different energy sources used in the United States. On a circle, or pie graph, such as this, the larger the section, or piece of the pie, the more that energy source is used. Use the graph to answer the questions.

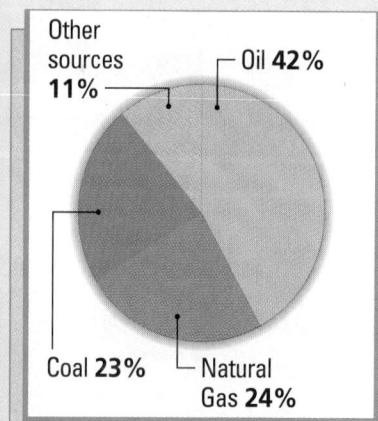

Other sources 11%

Oil 42%

Coal 23%

Natural Gas 24%

What Did You Find Out?
1. *Which energy source is used most?*
2. *Which energy source is used the least?*
3. *Which two energy sources are used about the same?*
4. *Which energy source is used most, oil or coal?*

Heat It Up!

Keeping warm air on the move

The rooms of a building get warm because the fire in the furnace heats the air in the furnace. Then the warm air is pushed through the ducts in the wall and into the rooms through open heat vents. The heated air moves through a room by convection. **Convection** is the flow of energy that occurs when warm air rises and cool air falls. The cold air vents on the walls allow cool air to return to the furnace. In the furnace, the cool air is warmed again and sent back through the house. In this way, the room and the rest of the house stay warm and cozy.

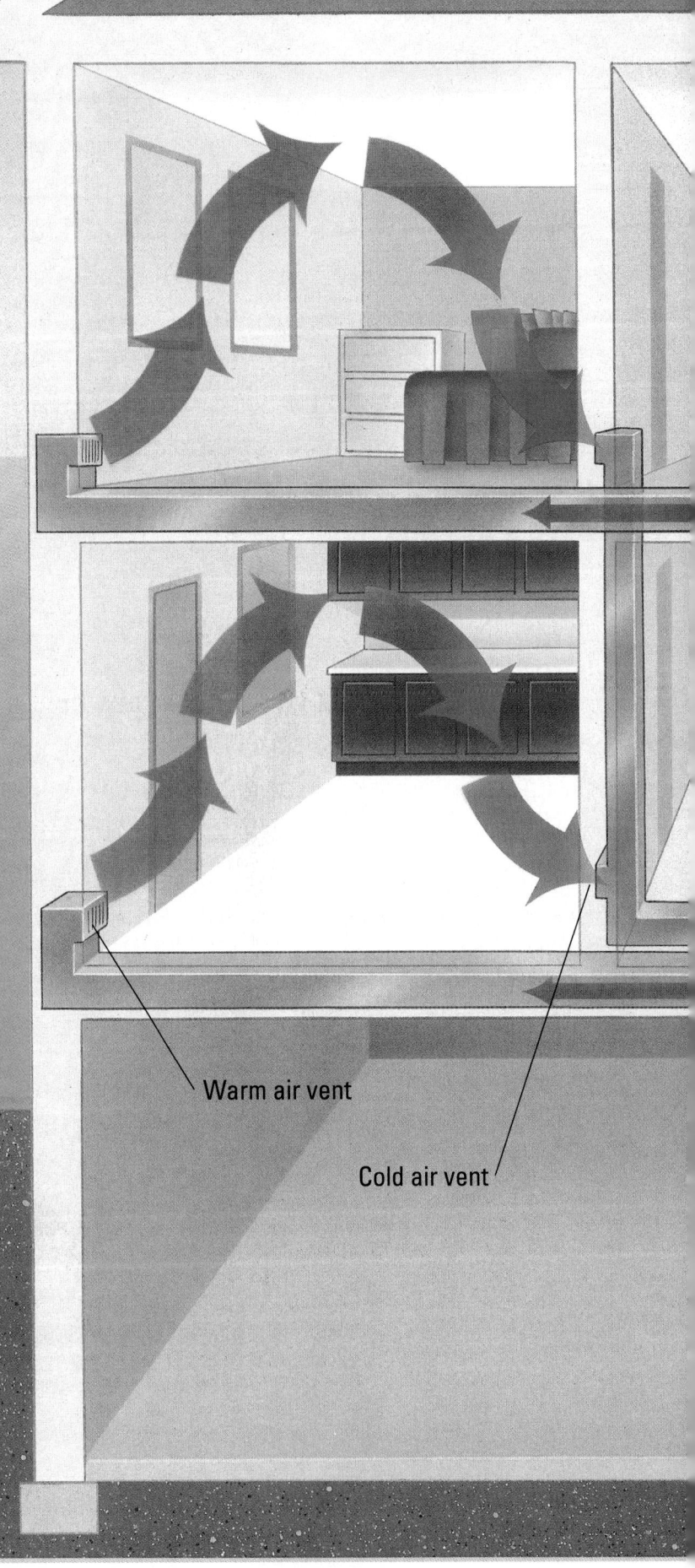

Warm air vent

Cold air vent

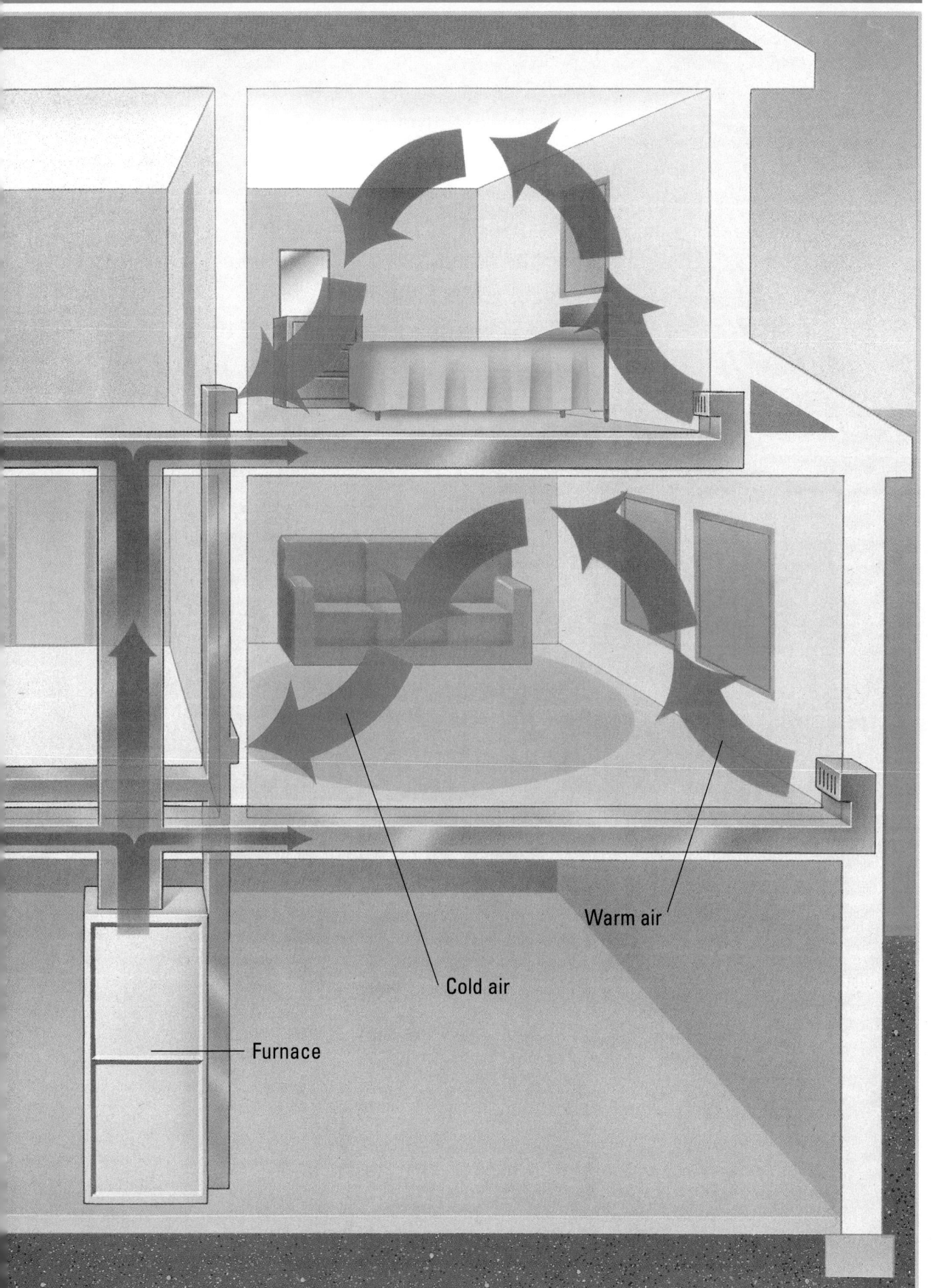

Warm air

Cold air

Furnace

Keeping Heat In or Out

People line their homes with insulators. Animals line their shelters with such natural resources as feathers and grass which are also good insulators. People and other animals have the same heating problem—how to keep the heat from escaping.

Since warm air rises, a lot of heat in a home escapes through the attic. To stop this heat loss, the man in the picture is putting insulation on the attic floor. He is using a fiberglass blanket that comes in rolls, as shown in the picture. Sometimes people pour or blow in pieces of fiberglass or other material between the floors and the ceilings or walls.

Heat can also be lost through and around the windows of a building. By covering windows with heavy drapes or shutters, heat loss can be cut down. Using storm windows also helps. Let's see how storm windows help to stop heat from escaping from a building.

▲ Insulation may also be put between the roof and the ceilings of rooms in a house.

➤ These windows also help keep heat from entering buildings in the summer.

Putting a storm window outside of a window leaves an air space between the two windows. Air, as a good insulator, helps keep heat from escaping. Look at the windows in the pictures. These windows help keep heat in without storm windows. The windows will have two or three panes of glass with air between the panes.

Buildings also can lose a lot of heat through holes or cracks around windows and doors. To seal these cracks, you can use felt, plastic, rubber, or other insulating materials. In a well-insulated home, you'll be as snug and warm in winter as the girl in the picture. Insulation keeps heat from escaping from a building. And it also keeps cold air from getting in. Insulation also keeps heat from entering a shelter, as in the hornet's nest. Therefore, in hot weather, insulation will help your shelter stay cool! By using insulation, less energy is needed to heat or cool homes.

▲ *Insulation in the walls and air between the window panes help keep the cold air out and warm air in.*

Into The Field

Can you find doors and windows that leak air?

Find a way to locate air leaks. Record what you discover.

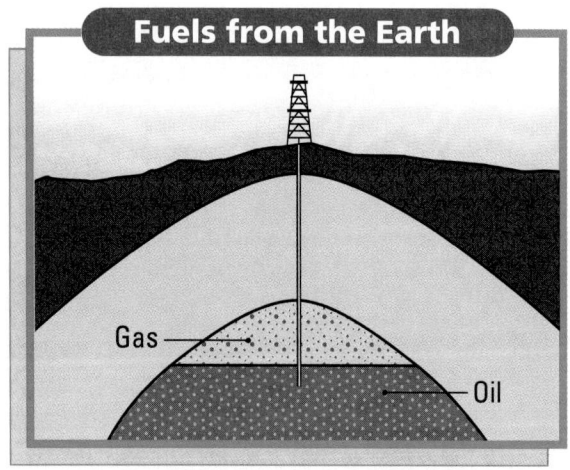

Fuels from the Earth

Gas —

— Oil

Fuel for Tomorrow

You're probably wondering why it's so important to insulate. It's important because the fuels used to heat and cool your home are limited natural resources.

Electricity is not a natural resource, but many power plants burn fossil fuels to produce electricity. Coal, oil, and gas are natural resources called fossil fuels. That's because they come from plants and animals that died millions of years ago. Look at the diagram showing where gas and oil are buried deep beneath the earth's surface. It takes millions of years for these resources to form.

No one knows how much oil, gas, and coal the earth contains. What is certain is the fact that at the rate people are using these fuels they will be gone soon. Most scientists predict that oil and gas will be used up in about fifty years. Coal supplies may last two hundred years more.

▼ *Coal can be mined from deep under the ground or from a strip mine.*

In time, new sources of fuel must be found as the world population grows. But for now, it is important to conserve fuel. To **conserve** fuel means to use resources carefully.

One way to conserve fuel is to use other sources of energy. Some people have built homes that are heated by energy from the sun— solar energy. Solar energy heats the house in this picture. Other houses make use of solar energy in another way. They have windows that face toward the south so a lot of sun shines into the house and warms it.

The best way people can conserve fuel is by insulating their homes. If a building is well-insulated, you burn less fuel to heat it. You also use less electricity to cool the building during hot weather. By using our resources wisely today, there will be more left for tomorrow.

▲ *The black collectors on this solar house absorb energy from sunlight to heat the house.*

Checkpoint

1. What are fossil fuels?
2. How does convection help heat move through a building?
3. How can people slow down heat loss from their homes?
4. Why is it important to conserve fuels?
5. **Take Action!** Find out from a family member what kind of fuel is used to heat your home.

Conserving Energy

Can windows with two panes help conserve energy? Try this activity using plastic bags to see what happens.

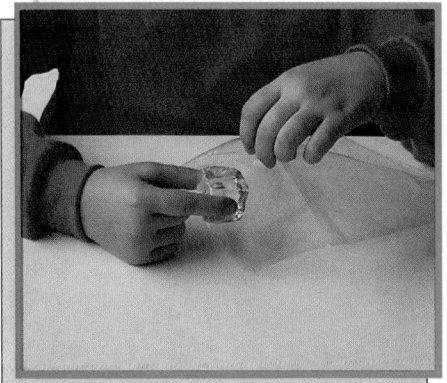

Picture A

Picture B

Picture C

Gather These Materials

cover goggles
small plastic bag
large plastic bag

2 ice cubes
2 small rubber bands
small dish

Follow This Procedure

1 Make a chart like the one on the next page. Record your results on your chart.

2 Put on your cover goggles.

3 Place an ice cube in the small plastic bag. (Picture A)

4 Seal the bag with a rubber band. (Picture B) *CAUTION: Be careful with the rubber band.*

5 Put the small plastic bag inside the large plastic bag. (Picture C)

6 Blow some air into the large plastic bag. Be careful not to burst the bag. Seal the bag.

7 Put the other ice cube in a small dish. Place the dish and the bag with the ice cube on a desk.

Predict: *What will happen to each ice cube?*

Record Your Results

	After 3 minutes	After 10 minutes
Ice cube in dish		
Ice cube in double plastic bags		

8 Watch what happens to each ice cube.

9 Describe what has happened to each ice cube after 3 minutes. Record what you see.

10 Record what the ice cubes look like after 10 minutes.

State Your Conclusions

1. What was the difference in the size of the ice cubes after 3 minutes? after 10 minutes?

2. Using what you know about heat and insulators, how do you explain the difference? Do you think windows with two panes of glass help conserve energy? Why or why not?

Let's Experiment

Do window curtains help conserve energy? Which kinds of curtains work best? Use what you know about scientific methods to find out.

Reading a Bar Graph

A graph shows data in a way that is clear and easy to read. A bar graph is a good way to compare several sets of data. Besides finding out numbers from a bar graph, you can also look quickly and see which bar shows the greatest amount or the least amount.

Thinking It Through

The graph to the right shows the number of birds' nests several children found on a nature walk. Notice the title of the graph and the labels. Also notice that the numbers are counted by twos. Graphs can be made using different numbering groups. Some graphs show the numbers by fives or even thousands!

To read a graph, use these steps:
1. Look quickly at the graph. Without reading the exact numbers, you can learn such things as who saw the most nests and who saw the fewest.
2. To find out how many nests a child saw, find the bar for that child. Then look at the numbers to the left of the graph. Look along the horizontal lines that mark each number. See which line the top of the bar reaches.

3. The bar doesn't always stop exactly on a line. If a bar stops between two numbers, the number it shows is the odd number between those two numbers. Notice that Lou's bar stops between 2 and 4. That means that Lou saw 3 nests.

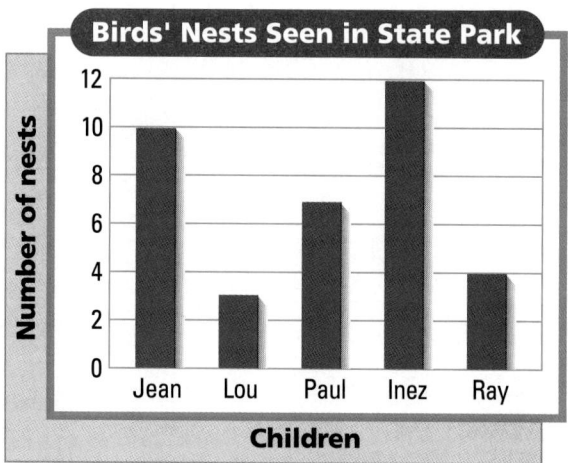

Your Turn

Use the graph to answer these questions:
1. Who saw the most nests?
2. Who saw the fewest nests?
3. Who saw 7 nests?
4. Which children saw more than 8 nests?

Chapter Review

Thinking Back

1. Why are the bodies of some animals always warm?

2. Compare an **insulator** and a **conductor**.

3. Explain how feathers or fur can help keep an animal warm.

4. What is a **fuel**? Name three fuels that people use today.

5. How does hot air get from the furnace to the rest of a house?

6. Explain how insulating houses helps **conserve** fuel.

Connecting Ideas

1. Copy the concept map. Use the terms at the right to complete the map to show how heat moves.

conductor   air
metal   convection

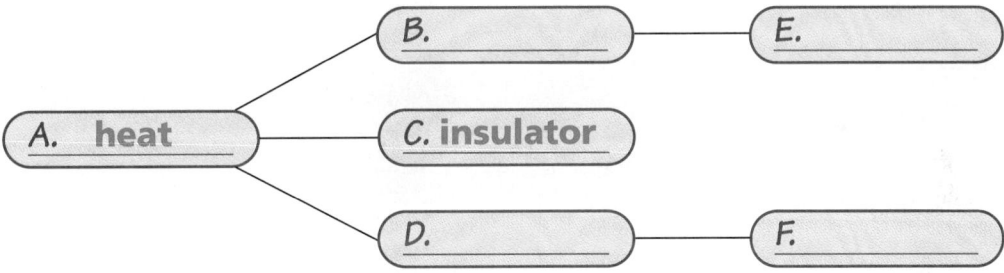

A. heat — B. _____ — E. _____
A. heat — C. insulator
A. heat — D. _____ — F. _____

2. Write a sentence or two about the ideas shown in the concept map.

Gathering Evidence

1. In the Activity on page 28, how did you know which material was the best insulator?

2. In the Activity on page 38, how did you conclude that air was a good insulator?

Doing Science!

1. **Design an activity** to show that snow is a good insulator.

2. **Make a chart** that shows different ways that people use insulators.

3

Machines in Building

Wear cover goggles for this activity.

How can you measure forces?

Cut a rubber band and pull on each end. Pull a little harder. What happens? Use a rubber band to measure force. Tie a piece of string to each end. Connect one end to a small box. Pull on the other end. Use the stretch of the rubber band to compare the force needed to move things.

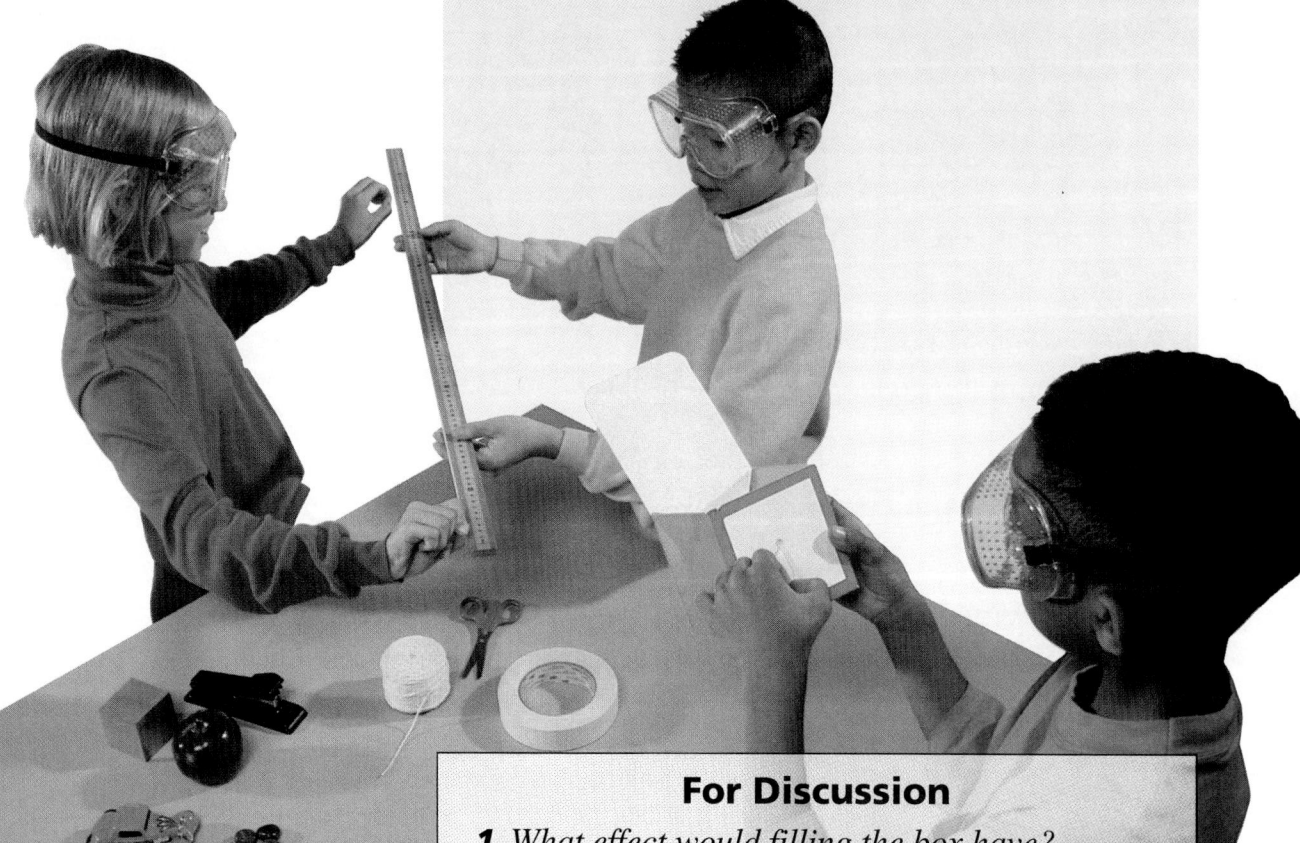

For Discussion

1. What effect would filling the box have?
2. What affects the force needed to move objects?

3.1 Simple Machines and Work

How do simple machines help people to build shelters?

You, too, can be a builder! Maybe you can't build a bird's nest or a beaver's lodge, but you can build a skyscraper. Does this idea sound impossible? With plastic blocks, you can build almost anything. These building blocks are light and snap together easily. You can join them in many different ways. Like the girl in the picture, all you need is time and imagination.

Building a real house is more difficult. Building materials are heavy and don't just snap together. You may need some tools to help you. Let's find out more about these tools and how they are used to help build shelters.

▼ What is the girl building with the plastic blocks?

Simple Machines

How are simple machines helpful in building a house?

Many tools are used to build a house. The six tools being used in the picture all use energy to do work. These tools are **simple machines**—machines with few or no moving parts. The wheelbarrow makes pushing heavy loads easy because its wheels are fastened together by an axle. Notice that the ramp is slanted so that the wheelbarrow moves up it easily. Nails are used to hold parts of the house together; sometimes screws are used instead. Why might a screw hold some things together better than a nail?

Nails are **wedges.**

The ramp is an **inclined plane.**

A **pulley** is used to lift large, heavy loads.

A **screw** is used to fasten things together.

The hammer is a **lever**.

The wheelbarrow has a **wheel and axle**.

What kind of a simple machine is the ladder that the roofer in the pictures is using?

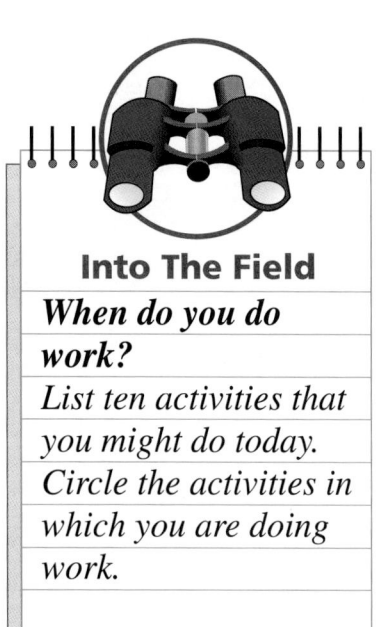

Into The Field

When do you do work?

List ten activities that you might do today. Circle the activities in which you are doing work.

Push, Pull, and Lift

No matter how helpful simple machines are, the builder still has to do work. Work is something we all do. When you sweep a floor, pick up a book, or throw a ball you are doing work.

What, then, is work? To find the answer, look at the pictures of the roofer. In each picture, something is moving. First the man picks up the shingles. Then he moves the shingles from the ladder to the roof and nails them in place. The shingles move because something makes them move. What makes them move? Remember from the Discover Activity that the something that makes objects move is force.

A **force** is a push or a pull. For example, the man pulls to pick up the shingles. The force makes the shingles move. The work is the lifting of the shingles. **Work** is something done whenever a force makes an object move through a distance. Simple machines make work easier because the work takes less force.

Work or No Work

You're doing work when you throw a ball. But suppose you try to lift a heavy bundle of shingles. You try, but no matter how much force—or energy—you use, you can't lift the shingles. Have you done any work? The answer is no! No matter how much force you use, you are doing no work unless the object moves. So if you don't move the shingles, you are doing no work. However, if you throw a ball, you're doing work because the ball moves.

Checkpoint

1. How do simple machines help in building shelters?
2. Where does the force come from when you pick up a book?
3. How do you know if you are doing work?
4. **Take Action!** Try to remove a nail from a piece of wood without and with a hammer. Explain the results.

Measuring Work

You know that it takes energy to do work. How much work can a marble do? Try this activity to find out.

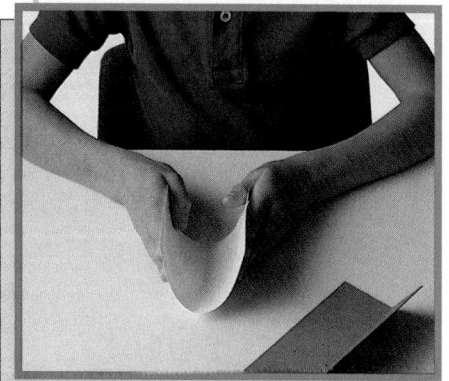

Picture A

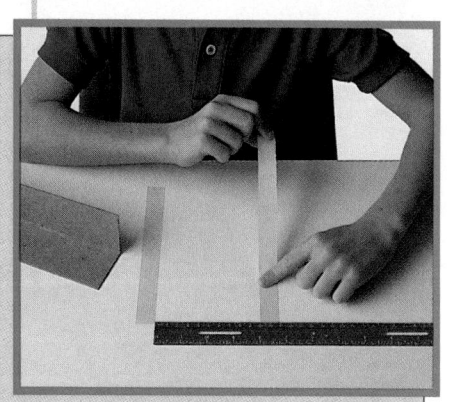

Picture B

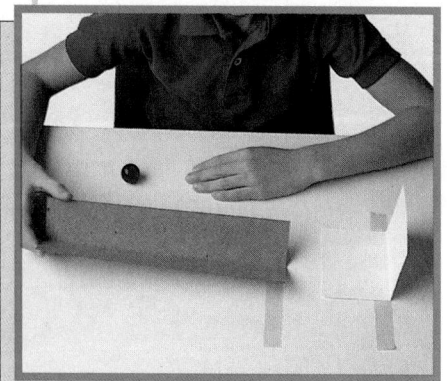

Picture C

Gather These Materials

piece of cardboard, 10 cm X 30 cm
file card

masking tape
metric ruler
marble

Follow This Procedure

1 Make a chart like the one on the next page. Record your results on your chart.

2 Fold the cardboard in half lengthwise. Fold the file card in half widthwise. (Picture A)

3 Stick two pieces of masking tape on a table top about 10 cm apart. Each piece of tape should be about 10–15 cm long. (Picture B)

4 Place the file card next to the tape on your left, so that one of the surfaces of the card lies flat on the table. Lay the folded edge of the card along the left edge of the tape.

5 Place one end of the folded cardboard next to the edge of the other piece of tape. Raise the opposite end of the cardboard 1 cm above the table top. (Picture C)

Predict: *What will happen when the rolling marble hits the file card?*

6 Place the marble at the top of the raised cardboard track. Then, let the marble roll down the track to hit the folded file card.

7 Measure how far the marble moved the file card. Record your results.

8 Repeat steps 4–7 three more times, with the end of the cardboard raised to 3 cm, 6 cm, and 9 cm above the tabletop. Measure how far the file card moves each time.

Record Your Results

Height	Distance card moved
1 cm	
3 cm	
6 cm	
9 cm	

State Your Conclusions

1. How high was the end of the track when the file card moved the farthest?

2. How did raising the cardboard track affect the results?

3. Using what you know about work and force, explain how the marble was able to do work.

Let's Experiment

Now that you have seen how a marble can do work, what would happen if you use a marble that is twice as big as the one you used? Use what you know about scientific methods to find out.

▲ One beaver may cut down more than two hundred trees in a year!

▼ Notice the sharp edge of the beaver's front teeth.

3.2 Animals' Simple Machines

▶ **What body parts of animals are used as simple machines?**

Have you ever seen a bird swing an ax or a rabbit use a shovel to dig a hole? Of course you haven't! Animals don't have the simple machines that people use. But animals do have body parts that they use in much the same way that people use simple machines.

Wedges and Levers

Remember how well the beaver in the picture can cut down trees. To see how, notice the beaver's front teeth in the picture. They are shaped like the chisel shown in the picture. The beaver uses its teeth in the same way that a carpenter uses a chisel or a lumberjack uses an ax. These workers use wedges to split wood apart, and to cut or make holes in an object. The beaver does the same with its front teeth.

Though they have a different shape than beavers' teeth, the beaks of some birds are also wedges. Look at the picture of the woodpecker's beak. The woodpecker has a beak that is shaped like a thin chisel such as the one in the picture. Using its beak, the woodpecker in the picture is chipping away at the wood to make a hole in the tree. Then the woodpecker will use the hole for a nest.

Most birds can also use their beaks like a pair of tongs that you might find in the kitchen. Tongs are really two levers fastened together at one end. Birds use their beaks in this way to pick up and carry materials they use to build their nests.

Think for a minute about the size of a carpenter ant or a termite. These tiny animals do not have teeth, but they have strong jaws. Their jaws are shaped somewhat like the beak of a woodpecker. They can chisel their way through a rotten tree or the wooden frame of a house with no problem. Carpenter ants make their nests in dead trees and old lumber. Many termites also carve out their tunnels in dead wood, and they often move into the wooden parts of a person's house.

▲ *The woodpecker is throwing chips of wood out of the hole it is chiseling.*

▼ *The woodpecker's beak and the chisel are tools that make work easier.*

Claws as Machines

Many animals use their claws as wedges and levers to build shelters. Rabbits, for example, have claws that are perfect for digging burrows in the ground. Look at the close-up of the rabbit's paw. Notice that each toe ends in a claw that is curved and pointed. Each claw is like a small wedge that the rabbit uses to loosen the soil. The claws are also like "built-in shovels." A shovel is a lever. To lift out the dirt, the rabbit uses its claws and hind feet like people use the shovel in the picture.

▼ *The rabbit scoops out a hole to build a nest.*

Gophers also use their claws as wedges and levers to dig tunnels for shelters. One gopher can make a 90-meter tunnel in a single night.

Bears have sharp, powerful claws and paws that they use as shovels or crowbars. Using its claws and paws as shovels, a bear can dig a shelter out of snow or soil. Some bears use caves as shelters. If a rock is blocking the opening to a cave, the bear can easily move the rock. To move a rock, a bear uses its paw, claws, and leg as a crowbar. Because their front paws do the work, the claws on the front paws are longer than the claws on the back paws.

Besides using its beak as a wedge, the woodpecker can also use its claws as wedges. Woodpeckers have two toes pointed forward and two toes pointed backward. Each toe ends in a long, sharp, curved claw. Each claw is like a tiny pick, or wedge, that can dig into tree bark and hang on. The claws help keep a woodpecker from falling off the tree while the bird pecks out a hole.

Checkpoint

1. How are the beaks and teeth of some animals like wedges?
2. How are a rabbit's claws like a wedge and a lever?
3. **Take Action!** Bite into an apple. Draw a picture of the teeth marks. What simple machine do they look like?

MATH

Size of Birds' Nests

Birds use their beaks, feet, and claws as wedges and levers to build nests. Birds build nests of all sizes and shapes. The graphs below show how the size of a bird's nest compares with the size of the bird. Use the graphs to answer the questions:

Bird	Height of Nest (cm)
Hummingbird	3
Osprey	183
Eagle	45

Bar graph. Vertical axis: Bird (Hummingbird, Osprey, Eagle). Horizontal axis: Height of Bird (cm), marked 10, 30, 50, 70, 90.

What Did You Find Out?
1. *How tall is an eagle? the eagle's nest?*
2. *How much taller is a hummingbird than the height of its nest?*
3. *Which of the three birds is tallest? Which nest is tallest?*
4. *How much taller is an eagle's nest than a hummingbird's nest?*

Activity

Beaks as Tools

Why do you think different birds have different kinds of beaks? Try this activity to find out how different kinds of beaks work.

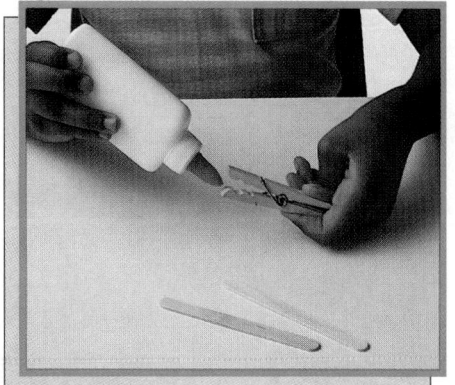

Picture A

Gather These Materials

cover goggles
pinch-type clothespin
glue
2 craft sticks, spoon,
    scissors, toothpick

10-12 pieces of each:
    uncooked macaroni,
    raisins, marbles,
    dry puffed cereal
small cup

Follow This Procedure

1 Make a chart like the one on the next page. Record your results on your chart.

2 Put on your cover goggles.

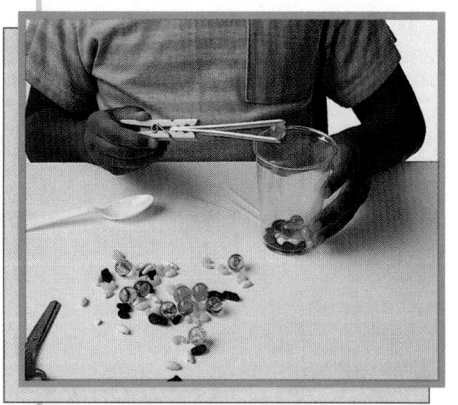

Picture B

3 Holding the clothespin open, glue the sticks inside the clothespin. (Picture A) When the glue dries, the clothespin works like a long beak. The clothespin, scissors, toothpick, and spoon will be used as "beaks" to pick up food.

4 Pretend these materials are different kinds of bird food: macaroni (worms), raisins (grubs), marbles (snails), and cereal (insects).

5 Scatter the "food" on a large table.

Picture C

Predict: *How well will each "beak" work as a food gathering tool?*

Record Your Results

	Macaroni	Raisins	Marbles	Cereal
Clothespin beak				
Scissors beak				
Toothpick beak				
Spoon beak				

6 Holding the clothespin at the pincer end, try to pick up and place in the cup as many pieces of "food" as you can in 2 minutes. (Picture B) Count how many pieces of each "food" you were able to pick up. Record your results. Empty the cup back onto the table.

7 Using the scissors like pincers, repeat step 6. Be careful with the scissors; keep them pointed down. (Picture C)

8 Repeat step 6 using the toothpick as a spear and then the spoon as a scoop. Use only one hand to get food with each "beak."

State Your Conclusions

1. Which "beak" worked best for getting different "food"?
2. Which "beak" would work better at crushing large seeds?

Let's Experiment

Now that you have seen how the "beaks" worked with these "foods," try picking up small bits of plastic foam floating in water.

Analyzing Facts

When you need to solve a problem, analyzing the information you have can help you. Information can be presented in many forms. These forms include bar graphs, maps, tables, and time lines.

Thinking It Through

Suppose you are reading about simple machines. You learn that a gear is a kind of wheel with teeth around the edge. Suppose you need to know when several different machines that use gears were invented.

Here are some ways to choose the information you need:

1. Think about what you need to know.

2. Think about what you can learn from a map, a graph, and so on.

3. Decide which kind of information would be most useful to you.

4. Look at the information given in the graph and the time line. You can see that the time line gives you the information you need.

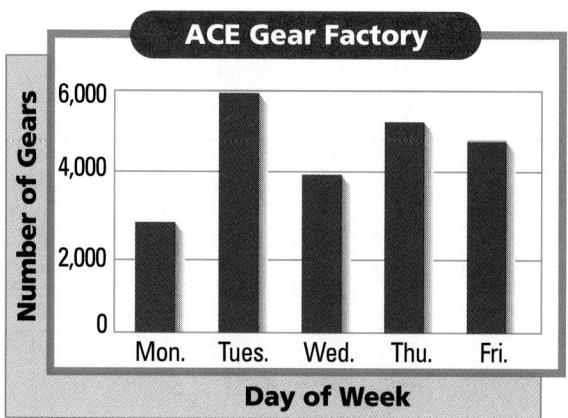

ACE Gear Factory

Your Turn

Look at the bar graph above. Write two questions about gears that you could answer from this bar graph.

Time Line

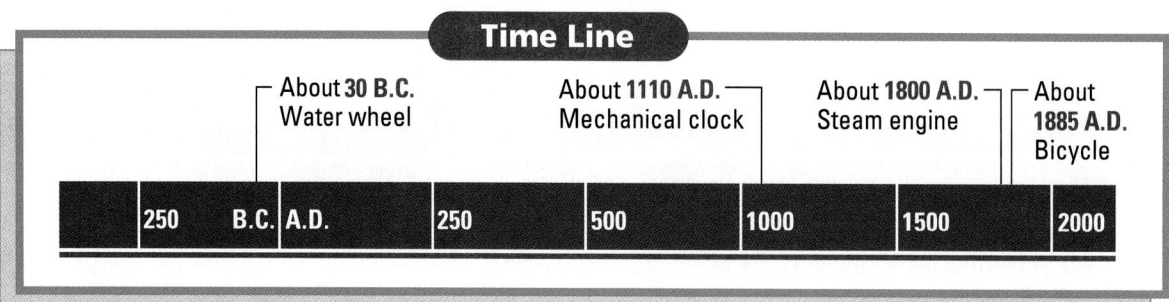

About **30 B.C.** Water wheel · About **1110 A.D.** Mechanical clock · About **1800 A.D.** Steam engine · About **1885 A.D.** Bicycle

| 250 | B.C. | A.D. | 250 | 500 | 1000 | 1500 | 2000 |

Chapter Review

Thinking Back

1. How are **simple machines** used to build a house?

2. How can an **inclined plane,** a **wheel and axle,** a **screw,** and a **pulley** be used in building?

3. Describe how a **force** can do **work.**

4. Explain why pushing hard on an object may not be work.

5. How does a beaver use its front teeth like a **wedge?**

6. How does a bear use its claws and legs as a **lever?**

Connecting Ideas

1. Copy the concept map. Use the terms at the right to complete the map to show how work is done.

work   **force**

movement

$$(\text{A.} \underline{\hspace{2cm}}) + (\text{B.} \underline{\hspace{2cm}}) = (\text{C.} \underline{\hspace{2cm}})$$

2. Write a sentence or two about the ideas shown in the concept map.

Gathering Evidence

1. In the Activity on page 48, how did you conclude that the height of the cardboard track changed the amount of work?

2. In the Activity on page 54, how did you conclude which "beak" was best at getting "foods"?

Doing Science!

1. *Design an activity* to show how a simple machine makes an object easier to move.

2. *Make a chart* to show which simple machines beaks, claws, paws, and legs work like.

Kid Inventor Beats the Cold

Chester Greenwood's ears made him famous. The only thing unusual about his ears was that they hurt when they got cold. This was a big problem for Chester because he grew up in Farmington, Maine. The winters there are very cold. But Chester found a way to beat the cold.

In 1873, Chester got ice skates for his fifteenth birthday. He rushed outside to try the skates on a frozen pond near his house. At first Chester had fun racing around on the ice. But before long his ears began to ache and he had to go back indoors.

The next time Chester wanted to go skating, he tied a wool scarf around his head. The scarf kept him warm, but it was so itchy that Chester didn't even get to the pond. What Chester needed was a way to keep only his ears warm. But what could he do?

Winters in Farmington, Maine, got very cold.

Then Chester had an idea—ear flaps! He bent pieces of wire into loops and had his grandmother sew fur on one side of the loop for warmth. She sewed velvet on the other side of the loop for softness. Then his grandmother used a wire to fasten the loops to Chester's cap. On his next trip to the pond, Chester found that his fur-covered ear flaps worked. His ears were warm at last.

Other people saw Chester's ear flaps and wanted some for themselves. Chester's grandmother and mother were soon busy making

lots of ear flaps for neighbors and friends.

At 19, Chester patented his invention. This means that he was on record as the inventor of earmuffs. Anyone who made and sold earmuffs would have to pay Chester a certain amount of money. As you may guess, Chester went into the earmuff business. He set up a factory in town and designed earmuff-making machines. He was on his way to making Farmington the earmuff capital of the world. Chester's inventing didn't stop at earmuffs.

The fur-covered ear flaps worked. His ears were warm at last!

He went on to make more than 100 other inventions. What is special about inventors like Chester? They do not have to go to college. And inventors don't even have to be adults! But whatever their age, inventors are curious. They want to know how things work. They are good at noticing problems, and they want to think of a way to solve them. You might be an inventor too.

On Your Own

Do you think that other things people use everyday were invented because someone had a problem? Try to find out who invented some other things that people use everyday—such as a light bulb, the telephone, or the radio. How were these things invented?

Outside with the Animals

Celina Gonzales

Occupation: Zoo Keeper
Hobbies: Horseback riding and playing with her dogs

When Celina was young, her parents were always telling her to come inside. If she had her way, she would stay outside all day long with her cats and dogs. Now Celina has her way. She stays outside all day with the animals at the San Antonio Zoo. Celina Gonzales is a zoo keeper.

What does a zoo keeper do?

"Mainly we feed and clean up after the animals. We also keep an eye on them in case they are sick or hurt."

Can you play with the animals?

"No, you always have to remember that the animals at the zoo are not tame. Zoo animals are wild. You never know when one of them might attack you. Some of the animals, like the squirrel monkeys, will jump on my back, and I feed them peanuts from my hand. But I would never pick them up or play with them—they might bite."

What do the animals eat?

"Most of them eat a prepared food called chow along with vegetables and fish. When I feed the animals, I move slowly and quietly so they don't get scared."

What's the best part of working at the zoo?

"I guess the best part is just getting to be outside, working with all of the animals. However, it is hard work. Cleaning up after the animals isn't that much fun. But cleaning is important—it helps keep the animals from getting sick. I really like taking care of the animals. And as I work with them, I am also learning more about them."

Solar Heating: Building Shelters

What happens to a sidewalk on a sunny day? It absorbs energy from the sun and gets warm. The sun's energy can be captured to use for warming homes. This process is called solar heating.

1 A flat metal plate called a solar collector, or solar panel, can be mounted on the roof to collect the sun's energy and become warm.

2 Many solar heating systems use water to heat the home; warm water moves through pipes inside the house.

3 The water is carried into a heat exchanger inside a water tank; this process warms a separate water supply used for bathing and washing.

4 The water circulates up through pipes into the collector; in the collector, heat from the panel warms the water.

Find Out On Your Own

Place a can covered with black paper and a can covered with white paper in the sun. Fill both with water and find out which will become warmer. Record the results.

Module Review

Making Connections

Energy

1. How do conductors and insulators affect the flow, or movement, of energy?

2. Why do we need to conserve fossil fuels and not solar energy?

Scale and Structure

3. How do animals and people build shelters to protect themselves?

4. Explain how animals are able to build shelters without the help of tools and machines. Give an example.

Diversity

5. What different kinds of natural resources do people use to build shelters?

6. Name the different sources of energy that people use to heat their homes.

Using What I Learned

Comparing

1. Compare the building of a beaver's lodge to the building of a person's house. How are they the same? How are they different?

2. Compare solar energy to a fossil fuel. How are they the same? How are they different?

3. Compare insulators and conductors.

Predicting

4. Suppose you built a snow house and sat in it for a half hour. Would you be warm or cold? Explain why.

Ordering

5. Make a time line from 1600 to today, marking each 100 years. Write the names of the fuels people commonly used to heat their homes during each time period.

Categorizing

6. Name two different kinds of simple machines. Give an example of an animal's body part that is used in somewhat the same way as each simple machine.

Observing

7. Look at the picture. Is work being done? Explain why or why not.

Applying What I Learned

Action Project
Talk to members of your family, your neighbors, and friends. Find out what actions they are taking to conserve natural resources. Share the information with your classmates. Report back good ideas from the class so that your family, neighbors, and friends can try them.

Drawing
Make a drawing of a house. Show where to insulate the house to prevent heat loss.

Performance Task
Use a ruler, an eraser, a small rock, and tape to make a model of a lever. Find out how to move the eraser so that you need the least amount of force to lift the rock.

Science Theater
Work with some classmates to write the words to a song about conserving natural resources. You may use music from a song you already know or compose your own. Teach the song to a group of friends and perform it for your class.

Exhibitions
Prepare a videotape, slide presentation, or photo exhibit to illustrate your thoughts about conserving natural resources.

What If
What if you were made principal of your school? What would you do to improve the school building? What would you do to conserve energy and other natural resources?

Using Metric

About 1 centimeter

About 1 millimeter

About 1 meter

Water boils (100°C)

Normal body temperature (37°C)

Water freezes (0°C)

1 cm

1 cm

1 square centimeter

1 cm

1 cm

1 cm

1 cubic centimeter

About 1 kilogram

Degrees Celsius

11 football fields end to end is about 1 kilometer

1 liter of milk

Using Scientific Methods

Scientists ask many questions. No one may know the answers. Then scientists use scientific methods to find answers. Scientific methods include steps like the ones on the next page. Sometimes scientists use the steps in different order. You can use these steps to do the experiments in this section.

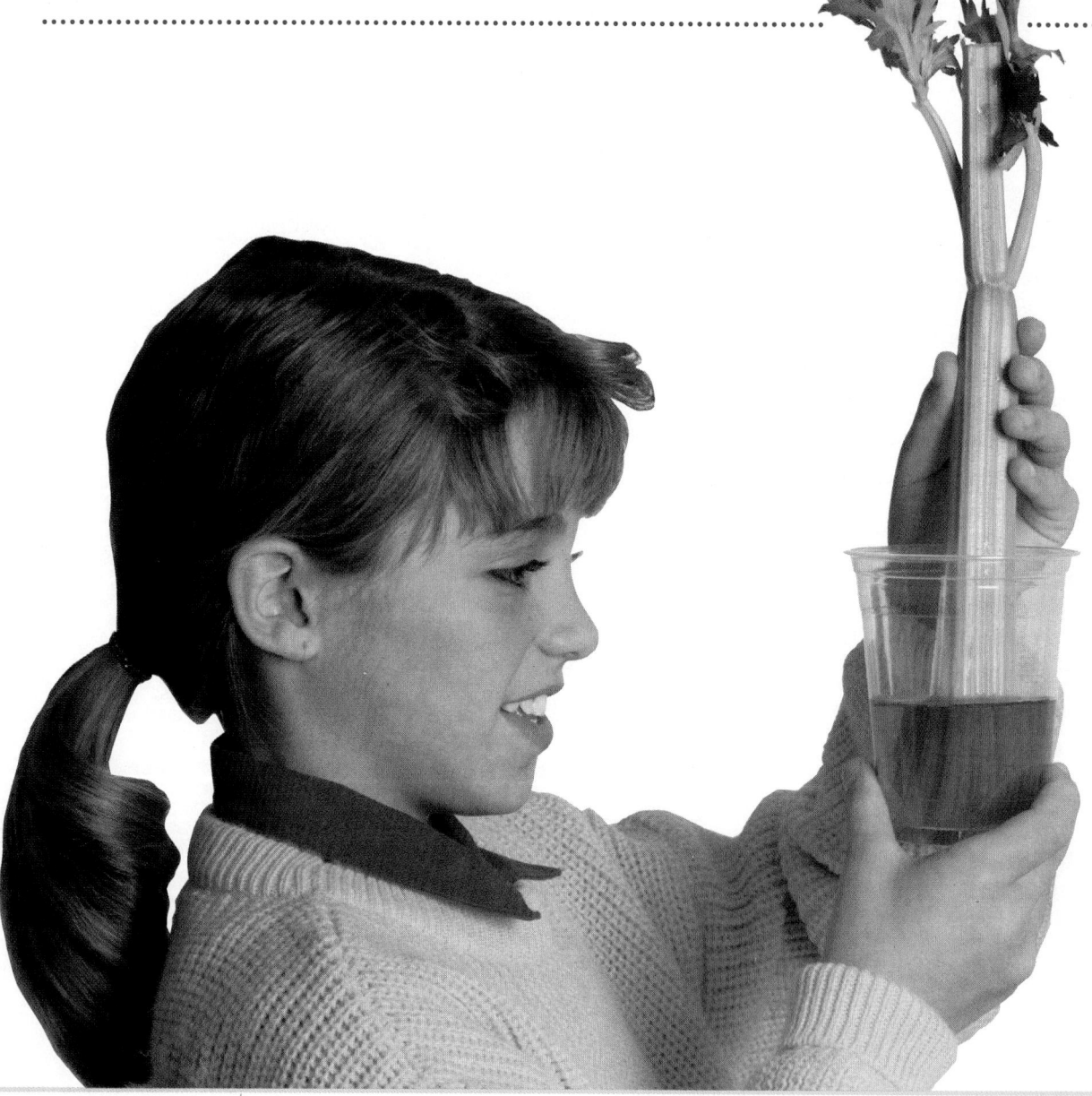

Test Hypothesis If possible, do an experiment to see if your hypothesis is correct. Then you should do the experiment again to be sure.

Collect Data Your observations from the experiment are your data.

Study Data You can understand your data better if you put it in charts and graphs.

Make Conclusions Decide if your hypothesis is correct.

Identify Problem The problem is usually a question such as, "Does sound travel faster through water than through air?"

Make Observations Notice many things about an object such as its size, color, or shape.

State Hypothesis Try to answer the problem.

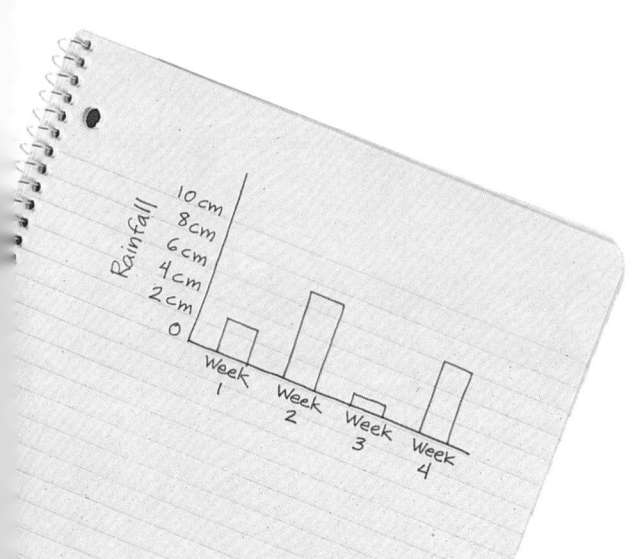

Safety in Science

Scientists are careful when they do experiments. You need to be careful too. The next page shows some rules to remember.

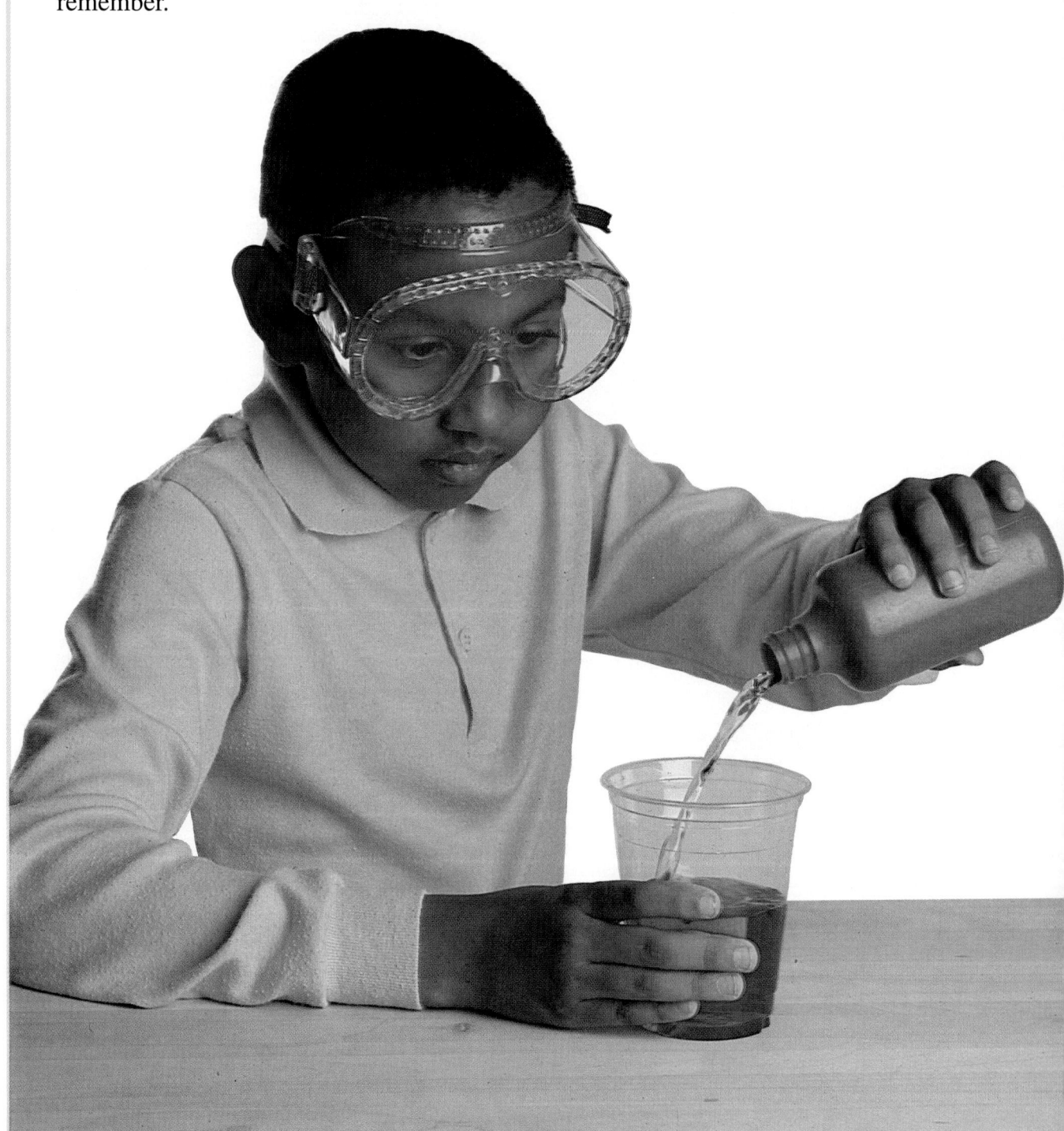

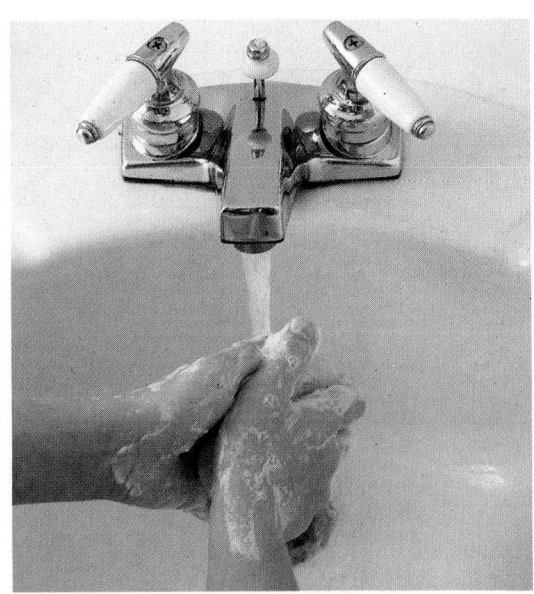

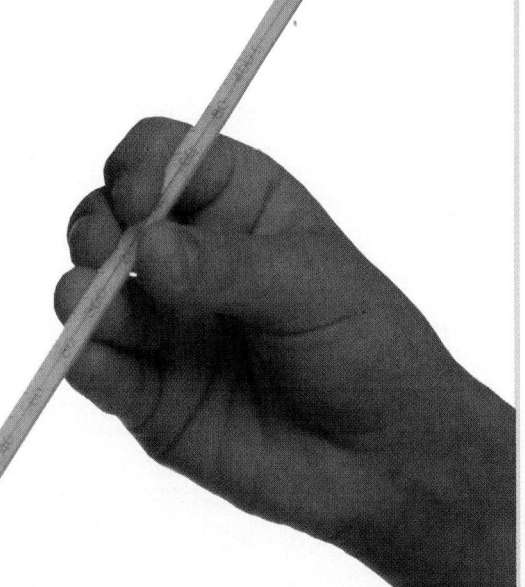

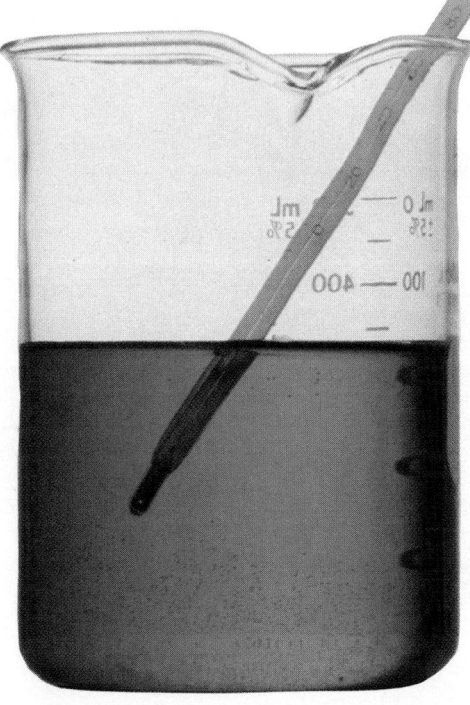

Safety Tips

- Read each experiment carefully.

- Wear cover goggles when needed.

- Clean up spills right away.

- Never taste or smell unknown things.

- Handle thermometers carefully.

- Put things away when you finish an experiment.

- Wash your hands after each experiment.

Making Observations

MODULE A

Experimenting with Mealworms

Tom liked visiting his uncle's farm. One day he noticed some tiny animals called mealworms. They were living in a damp sack of grain that an animal had spilled. Tom wondered if the mealworms like to live in a damp place or a dry place. He decided to do an experiment with ten mealworms to find out.

At the end of his experiment, Tom observed that only two of the ten mealworms crawled to a dry place. All the rest crawled to a wet place.

Thinking About the Experiment

1. Where did Tom first observe the mealworms?

2. What was Tom trying to find out in his experiment?

3. What materials did Tom use in his experiment? Check the materials list on the next page to find out.

Making observations means watching closely. Tom used his observations to make a conclusion.

4. How many mealworms did Tom observe at the dry place?

5. How many mealworms did Tom observe at the wet place?

6. What conclusion do you think Tom made?

Try It!

Try Tom's experiment and see if you come to the same conclusion.

Problem
Do mealworms prefer to live in a damp place or a dry place?

Hypothesis
Mealworms prefer to live in a damp place.

Materials
small cake pan   2 sponges
10 mealworms   water
cardboard   sand

Procedure
1 Fill the bottom of the pan with sand.

2 Wet 1 sponge. Then squeeze it.

3 Place the wet sponge in the sand on one side of the pan.

4 Place the dry sponge opposite the wet sponge.

5 Use a piece of cardboard to put the mealworms on the sand in the middle of the pan.

6 Observe the mealworms after 30 minutes. Write down how many are at each sponge.

Data and Observations

	Number of mealworms
Wet sponge	
Dry sponge	

Conclusion
Write your conclusion based on your data and observations.

Practice

Making Observations

1. Suppose you observed the mealworms for five days. Set up the data table that you would use.
2. Suppose you wanted to see if the mealworms grew. How could you make observations about growth?
3. What would you use to measure how much they grew?

Testing a Hypothesis

MODULE A

Experimenting with Heating Air

Nathan was keeping a weather chart as part of his science project. He noticed that the air seemed to get colder on clear nights than on cloudy nights. He wondered if clouds really affected the temperature of the air below them. He thought of this hypothesis as a possible answer to his question: *Covering air in some way helps keep it warm.*

Nathan did an experiment to test his hypothesis. He placed thermometers in two boxes. Then he covered both boxes and placed them in the sun for twenty minutes.

Thinking About the Experiment
Usually in an experiment, parts of the experiment take the place of things in nature. For example, the bottom of Nathan's shoe boxes act like the ground.

1. What does the plastic cover on the boxes take the place of?

2. Why did Nathan remove the cover from one of his boxes?

3. To test his hypothesis, did Nathan really need to remove the cover from one box? Why?

4. What do you think happened to the temperature of the air in each of the boxes?

Try It!
Try Nathan's experiment and see if you come to the same conclusion.

Problem
Do clouds help keep air warm?

Hypothesis
Covering air in some way helps keep it warm.

Materials
2 shoe boxes the same size
2 thermometers

plastic wrap
masking tape
60-watt bulb

Procedure
1 Place a thermometer in the bottom of 2 shoe boxes. Cover both with a double thickness of clear plastic wrap.

2 Set the boxes under a lighted bulb, about 10 cm from the bulb. Be careful, light bulbs can cause burns!

3 After 20 minutes, remove the plastic wrap from one of the boxes.

4 Record the temperature in each box every minute for the next 5 minutes. Do not remove the thermometers.

Data and Observations
Temperature of Air in Each Box

Time	Uncovered Box	Covered Box
0		
1		
2		
3		
4		
5		

Conclusion
Write your conclusion based on your data and observations.

Practice

Testing a Hypothesis
1. Suppose you wanted to do an experiment to find out if the color of the ground affects how fast air heats up. What would be your hypothesis?
2. How could you change Nathan's experiment to test your hypothesis?
3. What variable would change in testing this hypothesis?

Setting Up a Control

Experimenting with Plants

Marianne wanted to have colored glass put in her bedroom window. She had several plants in her room. She wondered if colored light coming in through the window would change how the plants grew. She decided to do an experiment with plants and red light to find out. In her experiment, Marianne found out that plants grow better in regular light than in colored light.

Thinking About the Experiment

1. Look at the materials list to find out how many cups Marianne used for her experiment.

Anything in an experiment that could change is called a variable. Only one variable should change during an experiment.

2. What variable did Marianne change between the two cups using cellophane?

3. Why was it important for the two cups to have all the same things except for the kind of cellophane?

The cup with a clear cellophane cone was the control in Marianne's experiment. It let in all light, just as clear glass would. Marianne could compare the plant from the control cup with the plant from the other cup.

4. Suppose Marianne did not have a control cup. Could she tell if the plant with red cellophane was growing any differently? Why or why not?

Try It!

Try Marianne's experiment and see if you come to the same conclusion.

Problem

How does red light affect bean seed growth?

Hypothesis

A bean plant will not grow as well in red light as in regular sunlight.

Materials

2 bean seeds	potting soil
cellophane, clear and red squares	stapler
	tape
metric ruler	water
2 plastic cups	

Procedure

1. Fill one of the cups with water. Soak 2 bean seeds in it overnight.

2. Empty the water from the cup. Fill both cups more than half full with potting soil.

3. Put a seed in each. Add a little soil on top of the seeds.

4. Water both cups well.

5. Make cones out of the two squares of cellophane. Use a staple to keep their shapes.

6. Tape a cone onto each cup.

7. Place the cups in a sunny spot.

8. After a week, measure the height of the plants. Count the number of leaves on each.

Data and Observations

	Red wrap	Clear wrap
Plant height		
Number of leaves		

Conclusion

Write your conclusion based on your data and observations.

Practice

Setting Up a Control

Plants need minerals to grow. Suppose you want to find out if plants grow better when minerals are added to the soil.

1. How would you change Marianne's experiment to find out how well plants grow with added minerals?

2. What would be the control in your experiment?

Setting Up an Experiment

Experimenting with Wedges

Jeff's father used a wedge to split wood. The hammer pushed the wedge into the wood and the wood split or cracked. Jeff wondered if the sharpness of a wedge makes a difference in how well it works. He decided to set up an experiment to find out. Jeff knew it was not safe to use his father's sharp wedge. He used wedges made out of chalk.

Thinking About the Experiment

Jeff set up his experiment carefully. He kept every part of the setup the same except for one variable. That was the variable he wanted to test.

1. What variable is Jeff testing?

2. Read the procedure to find out what variables Jeff kept the same in the experiment.

3. Predict how easy or hard it will be to push each of the chalk wedges into the clay.

Try It!

Try Jeff's experiment and see if you come to the same conclusion.

Problem

Does the sharpness of a wedge make a difference in how easily it can be pushed into something?

Hypothesis

A wedge is most useful if it has a sharp edge.

Materials

3 pieces of chalk
large ball of modeling clay
rough surface

Procedure

1. Rub one end of each piece of chalk on the rough surface to make a wedge shape. Make the ends of the wedges sharp, rounded, and flat.

2. Push each chalk wedge into the ball of clay.

3. Record how hard or easy it is to push each wedge.

Data and Observations

Wedge shape	Force needed
Rounded	
Flat-ended	
Sharp	

Conclusion

Write your conclusion based on your data and observations.

Practice

Setting Up an Experiment

Suppose you wanted to know if the material a wedge is made of affects how well it works.

1. What might be your hypothesis?
2. What variable would you test?
3. How would you set up your experiment?

Identifying Variables

Experimenting with Seeds

Pete was helping his mother plant seeds in the garden. He wondered if the seeds would germinate faster in warm weather than in cool weather. He did an experiment to find out.

Pete soaked 12 bean seeds in water overnight. The next day, he found a lid from a baby food jar and a lid from a peanut butter jar. He cut circles from a paper towel and put a circle in each lid. He put 10 drops of water and 4 bean seeds in the baby food lid. The peanut butter lid was much bigger, so he put 20 drops of water and 8 bean seeds in the peanut butter lid. Then Pete wrapped plastic wrap around the peanut butter lid and used a rubber band to keep the wrap in place. He put the lid in a warm, dark closet. He put the baby food lid in the refrigerator. He looked at the lids each day to see which seeds would germinate first.

Thinking About the Experiment

A variable is anything that can change in the experiment. Changing only one variable at a time tests for that variable. For example, using 20 drops of water in one lid and 10 drops of water in the other lid tests how the amount of water affects germination.

1. What did Pete first wonder about?

2. Should Pete use 20 drops of water in one lid and 10 in the other? Explain.

Pete did not set up his experiment correctly. He had too many variables that changed.

3. Explain how the lids Pete used were another variable that changed.

4. In addition to amount of water and lid size, Pete had two other variables that should not have changed. What were they?

Pete changed his experiment to keep all variables the same except one. Read Pete's new procedure on the next page.

5. How did Pete correct his procedure?

6. Which variable is Pete testing in the new procedure?

Try It!

Try Pete's experiment and see if you come to the same conclusion.

Problem
Does temperature affect how fast seeds germinate?

Hypothesis
Bean seeds will germinate faster in warm weather than in cold weather.

Materials
12 bean seeds
cover goggles
2 jar lids,
   same size
dropper
paper towel
plastic wrap
2 rubber bands
scissors
water

Procedure

1 Place 12 bean seeds in water and soak them overnight.

2 Use a jar lid to trace 2 circles on a paper towel. Then cut out the circles. Make sure the circles are the same size. Put 1 circle in each of 2 jar lids.

3 Put 10 drops of water and 6 bean seeds on the paper circle in each lid.

4 Cover each lid with plastic wrap. Use the rubber bands to hold the plastic wrap in place.

5 Put 1 lid in a warm, dark place. Put the other lid in a cold, dark place.

6 Observe the seeds each day for germination. Use a chart like the one below to record your observations.

Data and Observations

Number of seeds germinated		
	Warm	Cool
Day 1		
Day 2		
Day 3		
Day 4		
Day 5		

Conclusion
Write your conclusion based on your data and observations.

Practice

Identifying Variables

1. If you wanted to do an experiment to find out if bean seeds germinate faster in the dark than in the light, what variable should you test?

2. How would you change the experiment above to test this new variable?

Collecting Data

MODULE E

Experimenting with Sound

Ann tapped gently with a spoon on her glass of fruit juice. She was keeping time with music on the radio. Then she drank most of the juice. When she tapped the glass again she noticed that the sound was different. The sound was higher with less juice in the glass.

Ann wondered if this would be true if she tapped bottles. She thought of this hypothesis to answer her question. The more liquid in a bottle, the lower the sound made when you tap on the bottle. She decided to set up an experiment to test her hypothesis.

Thinking About the Experiment

In an experiment, you collect data about the problem you want to solve.

1. What is the problem in Ann's experiment?

2. What did Ann collect data about?

3. Look at the chart on the next page. How did Ann organize her data?

4. Make a prediction about whether Ann will hear a higher or a lower sound when more liquid is in the bottle.

Try It!

Try Ann's experiment and see if you come to the same conclusion.

Problem

Does the amount of liquid in a bottle make a difference in the sound made by tapping on the bottle?

Hypothesis

The more liquid in a bottle, the lower the sound made when you tap on the bottle.

Materials

4 bottles of the same size
water
spoon

Procedure

1 Put four bottles on a desk or table.

2 Leave the first bottle empty. Put a little water in the second bottle. Fill the third bottle about halfway. Fill the fourth bottle almost full.

3 Tap the first and second bottles gently with a spoon. Compare the sounds. Record which is higher.

4 Tap the third bottle. Compare the sound with the sounds of the first and second bottles. Record your observations.

5 Tap the fourth bottle and compare the sounds. Record your observations.

Data and Observations

Amount of water in bottle	Sound from tapping
Empty	
A little water	
Half full	
Full	

Conclusion

Write your conclusion based on your data and observations.

Practice

Collecting Data

Suppose you wanted to do an experiment to find out if the size of the bottle makes a difference in the sound produced.

1. What might your hypothesis be?
2. How could you set up an experiment to test the hypothesis?
3. What data is important to collect in your experiment?

Setting Up an Experiment

Experimenting with Fertilizer on Plants

Lori's grandmother lived on a farm with a big pond. A garden was near the pond. Lori noticed that the water nearest the garden looked greener than the rest of the pond. This water was covered with many tiny floating duckweed plants. Her grandmother said she used fertilizer in the garden. Lori wondered if the fertilizer had washed into the pond and made the duckweed near the garden grow quickly.

She set up an experiment using pond water, duckweed, and fertilizer to find out. In her experiment, Lori found out that duckweed with fertilizer grows faster than duckweed without fertilizer.

Thinking About the Experiment

1. What could Lori's hypothesis be?

2. Read the procedure on the next page. How many cups did Lori use to set up her experiment?

Lori made sure the cups she used were the same size. She put the same amount of pond water with duckweed in each cup. Then she put the cups in the sun. Lori changed one variable. This was the variable she was testing.

3. What variable did Lori change?

The cup without fertilizer was Lori's control.

4. How did the control help Lori with her observations?

Try It!

Try Lori's experiment and see if you come to the same conclusion.

Problem
Does fertilizer change how fast duckweed grows?

Hypothesis
Fertilizer helps duckweed grow quickly in water.

Materials
gloves
2 large plastic cups
marker
phosphate fertilizer
water with duckweed
medicine dropper

Procedure

1 Fill each cup half full with water.

2 Put on the gloves. Add 10 drops of fertilizer to one of the cups. Stir the fertilizer in the water.

3 Place 20 duckweed plants in each cup.

4 Record the number of plants in your data table beside "At start."

5 Label the cups. Put them in a sunny place.

6 Observe the cups once a week for two weeks. Count the duckweed plants in each cup each time. Record the numbers on your data table.

Data and Observations

	With fertilizer	Without fertilizer
At start		
After 1 week		
After 2 weeks		

Conclusion
Write your conclusion based on your data and observations.

Practice

Setting Up an Experiment
Does the temperature of water affect how fast duckweed plants grow? Suppose you wanted to set up an experiment to find out. You could use two cups of pond water with duckweed.

1. What would be the same about each cup?
2. What would be the variable?
3. What would be the control?

Glossary

A

absorb (ab sôrb′), to take in.

algae (al′jē), a group of producers that live in water.

amplify (am′plə fī), make stronger.

antenna (an ten′ə), one of the feelers on the heads of insects and other animals.

B

blood vessel (ves′əl), any of the tubes in the body through which blood circulates.

bran (bran), the outer covering of a seed of grain.

bullhorn (bu̇l′hôrn′), a megaphone with a microphone that acts as a loudspeaker.

bur (bėr), a fruit that has seeds inside and hooks that cling.

C

calcium (kal′sē əm), a mineral in foods that helps keep teeth and bones strong.

carbohydrate (kär′bō hī′drāt), a nutrient that the body uses for energy.

clay soil, tightly packed soil with tiny grains.

cloud (kloud), condensed water droplets or ice particles floating in the sky.

community (kə myü′nə tē), all organisms that live in a place.

condensation (kon′den sā′shən), the changing of a gas to a liquid.

condense (kən dens′), to change from a gas to a liquid.

conductor (kən duk′tər), a material through which energy moves easily.

conserve (kən sėrv′), to save or keep from harm.

consumer (kən sü′mər), a living thing that depends on producers for food.

contract (kən trakt′), the action of a muscle becoming shorter.

control (kən trōl′), the part of an experiment that does not have the variable being tested.

convection (kən vek′shən), the flow of energy that occurs when a warm liquid or gas rises.

D

decompose (dē′kəm pōz′), break down a substance into what it is made of.

desert (dez′ərt), a dry habitat.

digest (də jest′), to change or break down food into forms the body can use.

disposable (dis pō′zə bəl), that which can be thrown away after use.

E

eardrum, the thin skin at the end of the ear canal.

echo (ek′ō), a sound that bounces back.

electric signal (i lek′trik sig′nəl), a form of energy.

embryo (em′brē ō), the tiny part of a seed that can grow into a plant.

endangered (en dān′jərd) **living things,** kinds of living things that are very few in number and might someday no longer be found on the earth.

energy (en′ər jē), the ability to do work.

environment (en vī′rən mənt), everything that surrounds a living thing.

evaporate (i vap′ə rāt′), to change from a liquid to a gas.

evaporation (i vap′ə rā′shən), the changing of a liquid into a gas.

exoskeleton (ek′sō skel′ə tən), a hard covering that supports the body of some animals.

extinct (ek stingkt′), no longer found living on the earth.

F

fat (fat), nutrient the body uses for energy.

fertilizer (fėr′tl ī′zər), a substance spread over or put into the soil to supply missing nutrients.

fiber (fī′bər), a part of foods that cannot be digested.

food chain, the way energy passes from one living thing to another in a community.

force (fôrs), a push or a pull.

forest (fôr′ist), a large area of land that gets plenty of rain and is covered with many trees.

fossil fuel (fos′əl fyü′əl), a fuel, such as oil, natural gas, or coal, that was made from living things that died millions of years ago.

fruit (früt), a covering that protects seeds made by flowering plants.

fuel (fyü′əl), any material that can be burned to produce useful heat.

G

gasoline (gas′ə lēn′), a fuel made from petroleum and used in heat engines.

germinate (jėr′mə nāt), to begin to grow and develop.

H

habitat (hab′ə tat), the place where a living thing lives.

hibernate (hī′bər nāt), to spend the winter in a state in which the body greatly slows down.

humus (hyü′məs), the decayed matter in soil.

hypothesis (hī poth′ə sis), a likely explanation of a problem.

I

incinerate (in sin′ə rāt′), to burn to ashes.

inclined (in klīnd′) **plane,** a simple machine that is a flat surface with one end higher than the other.

insulator (in′sə lā′tər), a material through which energy cannot easily flow.

iron (ī′ərn), a mineral in foods that is needed for good health.

J

joint (joint), a place where bones join together; different joints allow different movement.

L

large intestine (in tes′tən), an organ of the digestive system that removes water and stores waste material until it leaves the body.

lever (lev′ər), a simple machine made of a bar that is held up on a point called a fulcrum.

loam (lōm), soil that is a mixture of clay, sand, and humus.

M

matter (mat′ər), substance of which all objects are made.

megaphone (meg′ə fōn), a large, funnel-shaped horn or similar device, used to increase the loudness of the voice or the distance at which it can be heard.

membrane (mem′brān), a thin layer of skin that covers, separates, or connects some parts of the body.

migrate (mī′grāt), to move from one place to another when the seasons change.

mineral (min′ər əl), a material that was never alive and that can be found in soil; a nutrient the body needs in small amounts to work properly.

N

natural resource (nach′ər əl ri sôrs′), something people use that comes directly from the earth.

nerve (nėrv), a body part that carries messages to and from the brain.

nonrenewable resource (non′ri nü′ə bəl ri sôrs′), a resource that cannot be replaced once it is used up.

nutrient (nu′trē ənt), a material that plants and animals need to live and grow.

P

petroleum (pə trō′lē əm), a liquid deep in the ground that was made from living things that died millions of years ago.

photosynthesis (fō′tō sin′thə sis), the process by which plants make sugars.

pitch (pich), how high or low a sound is.

pollution (pə lü′shən), anything harmful added to the air, water, or land.

population (pop′yə lā′shən), living things of the same kind that live in the same place.

precipitation (pri sip′ə tā′shən), moisture that falls to the ground.

producer (prə dü′sər), a living thing that makes sugars.

protein (prō′tēn), a nutrient that the body uses for growth and repair.

R

recycle (rē sī′kəl), to change something so it can be reused.

reflect (ri flekt′), to bounce back.

S

saliva (sə lī′və), the fluid in the mouth that makes chewed food wet and begins digestion.

sandy soil, loose soil with large grains.

sanitary (san′ə ter′ē) **landfill,** a place where garbage is dumped and covered with soil.

screw (skrü), a simple machine used to hold objects together.

scrubber (skrub′ər), a device attached to a smokestack designed to remove harmful materials.

seed coat, the outside covering of a seed.

seedling (sēd′ling), a young plant that grows from a seed.

sewage (sü′ij), waste water and human wastes.

shelter (shel′tər), something that covers or protects from weather, danger, or attack.

simple machine, any of six kinds of tools with few or no moving parts that make work easier.

skeleton (skel′ə tən), the bones of a body.

sleet (slēt), partly frozen rain.

small intestine (in tes′tən), the organ of the digestive system in which most digestion takes place.

solar (sō′lər) **energy,** energy that comes from the sun.

sound, the energy of vibrating matter.

state of matter, the form that matter has—solid, liquid, or gas.

stomach (stum′ək), the organ of the digestive system that receives food after it is swallowed.

T

temperature (tem′pər ə chər), a measurement of how hot or cold matter is.

tendon (ten′dən), a ropelike part of the body that holds a muscle to a bone.

theory (thē′ər ē), one or more related hypotheses supported by data that best explains things or events.

thermometer (thər mom′ə tər), an instrument for measuring temperature.

transportation (tran′spər ta′shən), means of moving from one place to another.

V

variable (ver′ē ə bəl), anything in an experiment that can be changed.

vibrate (vī′brāt), to move quickly back and forth.

vitamin (vī′tə mən), a nutrient the body needs in small amounts to work properly.

vocal cords (vō kəl′ kôrdz), thin flaps at the top of the windpipe.

volume (vol′yəm), loudness or softness of a sound.

W

water cycle (sī′kəl), the movement of water by evaporation, condensation, and precipitation.

water pollution (pə lü′shən), anything harmful added to water.

water vapor (wô′tər vā′pər), water in the form of a gas.

wedge (wej), a simple machine used to cut or split an object.

wheel and axle (hwēl and ak′səl), a simple machine that has a center rod attached to a wheel.

wildlife refuge (ref′yüj), place of safety or security for wild animals and plants.

work (wėrk), the result of a force moving an object.

Index

Conductors, C26
Conservation
  of fuel, D58
  of energy, C38-39
  of resources, C37
Consumers, B15-17
Contraction, muscle, D11
Convection, C32-33

D

Darling, J. N. "Ding," F53
Decomposition, of garbage, F25-26
Deserts, A4-39
  animals in, A10, A12-17
  habitats in, A7, A8-9
  at night, A16-17
  plants in, A10-11
  rain in, A30-35
  shelter in, A14-15
  Sonoran, A5-35
  water in, A4-9
Digestion, B51-53

E

Eardrum, E33
Earmuffs, C58-59
Ears
  animal, E34
  parts of, E32-39
Earth. *See also* Pollution; Soil
  environmental protection and, F38-61
  and garbage, F20-36
  protecting the, F4-63
  water resources, F5-18
Earthworm, D15, D16-17, D26-27
Echoes, E18-19, E22
Edison, Thomas, D45
Electricity, C31, C36
  and sound, E7
Electric signals, E49

Embryo, B6
Endangered animals, F43-46
Energy. *See also* Electricity; Fuels; Sun
  conservation of, C38-39
  electric, E50-51
  from food, B14-15
  plants and B4-21
  sound, E6
  sources of, C31
  steam, D45
  and transportation, D40-41
  and work, C48
Engines, D46-47
Environment, F39-41
Evaporation, A34, A36-37, B33
Exoskeletons, D15
Extinction, of animals, F46-47

F

Factories, and water pollution, F15
Farmers, and water pollution, F14
Fat, B47, B48-49
Fertilizers, F14
Fiber, B42
Fish, E37
  movement of, D12
  and water pollution, F10-11
Food chain, B16-17, B18-19
  pollutants in, F9
Foods, B39-47
  in cities, A52
  digestion of, B51-53
  energy from, B14-17
  five food groups, B44-45
  in forest habitat, A47
  groundwater and, F16-17
  healthful, B44-45, B46-47
  and movement, D21-25
  from plants, B10
  snack, B48-49

Force, C46
   measuring, C42
Forest rangers, A60
Forests, A40-53, A60
   animals in, A43, A46-49, A50-51
   kinds of, A42
   lumber and, C6-7
   plants in, A43, A46-49, A50-51
   rain in, A41-42
   winter in, A48-49
   in Wisconsin, A43
Fossil fuels, C36
Freezing, A48. *See also* Ice
Fruits
   seeds and, D6, D8
   and vegetables, B40-41
Fuel, C30-37
   conservation and, C36-37, D58-59

G

Garbage pollution, F20-36
Garbage trucks, F61
Garden, location of, B23
Gardening, B4-63
   plants and energy, B4-21
Gas
   gasoline, D48-49
   natural, C31, C36
Germinate, B6, B7, B11
Greenwood, Chester, C58-59
Groundwater, and food, F16-17

H

Habitats, A7, A50-51
   changing, F42-47
   city, A52-53
   desert, A7, A8-9
   forest, A41-45
   protection of, F50-53
   water, F8

Hearing, E32-39
Hearing aids, E52-53
Heat
   in desert, A23-27
   fuels and, C30-37
   insulation and, C34-35
   insulators, C26-27
   materials as, C28-29
How Things Work
   garbage truck, F61
   levitating train, D61
   peppermint oil, extracting, B61
   solar heating, C61
   thermometer, A61
   trombone, E61

I

Intestines, B52-53
Inventors
   Bell, Alexander, E56
   Edison, Thomas, D45, E56
   Greenwood, Chester, C58-59
Iron, C10

J

Joint, D11

L

Land, changing, F39-41. *See also* Earth
Landills, F60
Leaves, A42, A43
Levers, C45
   of animals, C50-51, C52-53
Light energy, A24-25
Limestone, C11
Liquid, A48
Living things
   energy from, D40
   in water, F8-9
Lizards, in desert, A12-13

Loam, B27
Lodges, beaver, C16-17
Log cabin, C18
Loudness, and noise pollution, E58-59
Lumber, C6-7

M

Machines, C43-54
  and transportation, D40
Mass-transit system, D52
Materials, heating of, A28-29
Matter, A24
  states of, A48
Meats and milk products, B43
Medicine, from plants, B61
Megaphones, E44-45
Mexicans, and shelters, C19
Microphones, E50-51
Migration, D28-34
  in air, D32-33
  on land, D28-29
  in water, D30-31
Milk
  changes in, B54-55
  products, B43
Minerals, B41
Mining, C10, C36
Movement, D4-63
  of animals, D28-37
  of birds, D20
  energy for, D10
  migration, D28-34
  of people, D38-59, D61
  of seeds, D5-9
  for survival, D20-36
  in water, D30-31

N

Nails, C10-11
Native Americans, shelters of, C18-19

Natural gas, C31, C36
Natural resources, C7
  animal shelters and, C14-17
  as building materials, C8-9
  conservation of, C37, D58-59
  as insulators, C34
  petroleum as, D51
  and shelters, C14-17, C27
  water as, F5-7
Needle-like leaves, A42
Nerves, E33
Nests, C14-15, F54-55
  of birds, C53
  building, C20-21
Newspapers, recycling of, F34-35
Noise pollution, E58-59
Nonrenewable resource, D51
Nutrients, B24, B39. *See also* Foods

O

Oil, C31, C36
  and gasoline, D48-49
Oil spill, F4

P

People
  effect on plants and animals, F42-47
  movement of, D10-11, D38-59, D61
Pesticides, F14, F18
Petroleum, D45, D51
  and gasoline, D48-49
Photosynthesis, B14-15
Pitch (of sound), E12-13, E33, E61
Plants. *See also* Seeds
  in desert, A10-11, A31, A32-33
  and energy, B4-21
  in forests, A43, A46-49, A50-51
  medicine from, B61
  people and, F42-47
  protecting, F50-53

Steel, C10
Stomach, B52
Sugars, B10, B47
Sun
   and evaporation, A34, A36-37
   and garden, B23
   heating by, A24-28
   and temperature, A23-27
Survival. *See also* Deserts
   in desert, A10-17
   and hearing, E34-35
   movement for, D20-36
   and rainfall, A5

T

Telephone, E7, E50
Temperature, A22
   in desert, A23-27
   finding, A38
   and heat movement, C24
   measuring, A26-27
Tendons, D11
Thermometer, A26-27
   reading, A61
Tools, C44
   beaks as, C54-55
Trains, D52, D61
Transportation, D29-41
   effects of, D50-51
   energy use for, D46-47, D48-49
   pollution and, D52-53
Trash pollution, F20-36
Travel
   and fuel used, D51
   in past, D39-41
   in present, D44-45
Trees. *See also* Forests; Lumber
   mesquite, A5
   protecting, F50
Trombone, E61
Tuning fork, E46-47

U

Urban horticulturalist, B60

V

Vegetables. *See* Fruits and vegetables
Vibration, E12
   and ear, E33
   and sound, E6-7
Vitamins, B40-41
Vocal cords, E26-27
Volume (sound), E10-11

W

Wastewater treatment, F12-13
Water, F5-7. *See also* Rain
   in cities, A52
   in desert, A4-9, A12, A18-19
   on the earth, B30-34
   in forest, A42, A47
   forms of, A48-49
   and movement, D24-25, D30-31
   pollution of, F8-9, F12-18
Water cycle, B32-33, B34-35
Water energy, D41
Water pollution, F8-9, F12-18
Water vapor, A34, A48, B30
Wedges, C44
   of animals, C50-51, C52-53
Wheels and axles, C45
Wildlife refuges, F52-53
Wind energy, D6, D41
Winter
   in forests, A48-49
   and migration, D36
Wood, as fuel, C30-31. *See also* Lumber;
   Trees
Work, C46-47

Acknowledgments

ScottForesman

Editorial: Terry Flohr, Janet Helenthal, Mary Ann Mortellaro, Kathleen Lally, Dorothy Murray, Glen Phelan, Matthew Shimkus

Art and Design: Barbara Schneider, Jacqueline Kolb, George Roth, Cathy Sterrett

Picture Research/Photo Studio: Nina Page, Rosemary Hunter, Judy Ladendorf, John Moore

Photo Lab/Keyline: Marilyn Sullivan, Mark Barberis, Gwen Plogman

Production: Barbara Albright, Francine Simon

Marketing: Lesa Scott, Ed Rock

Ligature, Inc.
Pupil Edition interior design and production

Unless otherwise acknowledged, all photographs are the property of ScottForesman. Unless otherwise acknowledged, all computer graphics by Ligature, Inc. Page abbreviations are as follows: **(T) top, (C) center, (B) bottom, (L) left, (R) right, (INS) inset.**

Module A
Photographs
Front & Back Cover: Background: Tom Algire/Tom Stack & Associates Children's Photos: Allan Landau for ScottForesman

Page A2(C) Larry Ulrich/DRK Photo **A3(T)** C.Allan Morgan/ Scott, Foresman **A3B** Don and Pat Valenti **A5** Mike Price/ Bruce Coleman, Inc. **A6-7** Stephen J Krasemann/Peter Arnold, Inc. **A10** Larry Ulrich/DRK Photo **A11** Larry Ulrich/DRK Photo **A12** C.Allan Morgan **A13** John Cancalosi/DRK Photo **A14(T&B)** C.Allan Morgan **A15(T)** Jeff Foott/Tom Stack & Associates **A15(B)** C.Allan Morgan **A16(T)** C.Allan Morgan **A16(B)** John D Cunningham/Visuals Unlimited **A17** John J.Hoffman/Bruce Coleman, Inc. **A23** Robert & Linda Mitchell **A24** Don & Esther Phillips/Tom Stack & Associates **A25** Martin W Grosnick/Bruce Coleman, Inc. **A26(T)** Robert & Linda Mitchell **A26(B)** Breck P.Kent **A30** T.A.Wiewandt **A31** T.A.Wiewandt/DRK Photo **A32(T&B)** C.Allan Morgan **A33(T&B)** C.Allan Morgan **A34** T.A.Wiewandt **A35** David Muench **A41, A42(B), A43(B), A46** Don and Pat Valenti/f/stop **A47(T)** Rod Planck **A48(TL)** Rod Planck **A48(BL)** Leonard Lee Rue III/Bruce Coleman, Inc. **A48(R)** Don and Pat Valenti/ f/stop **A50(TL)** Robert & Linda Mitchell **A50(BL)** Tom Algire/Tom Stack & Associates **A50(CR)** Nancy Adams/Tom Stack & Associates **A50(BR)** C.Allan Morgan **A51(T)** Tom Algire/ Tom Stack & Associates **A51(B)** Don & Pat Valenti/ f/Stop Pictures, Inc. **A56(B)** Rannels/Grant Heilman Photography **A56(T)** Grant Heilman Photography **A58(T)** Ed Kashi **A58(B)** Allan Roberts **A59** Courtesy of Pamela McKinnon, Goldendale, WA. **A60** Delwin Price

Illustrations
Page A2 Carla Simmons **A12-13** Mark Langeneckert **A32-33** Carla Simmons **A61** Rich Lo

Module B
Photographs
Front & Back Cover: Children's Photos: Allan Landau for ScottForesman

Page B3(BL) Alex S.MacLean/Landslides **B11(T)** Milt & Joan Mann/Cameramann International, Ltd. **B16** Carlyn Galati/Visuals Unlimited **B27** Alex S.MacLean/Landslides **B30(ALL)** Warren Faidley/Weatherstock **B31(L)** Warren Faidley/Weatherstock

Illustrations
Page B3(T) Karen Kluglein **B3(B)** Rolin Graphics **B6(T)** Rolin Graphics **B8-9** Wild Onion Studio **B10** Karen Kluglein **B14-15** Elizabeth Allen **B16-17** Elizabeth Allen **B20** Joe Rogers **B24-25** Ebet Dudley **B41** Karen Kluglein **B44-45** Ron Becker **B52** Michael Schenk **B56** Joe Rogers **B61** Steve Fuller

Module C
Photographs
Front & Back Cover: Background: William J.Weber/ Visuals Unlimited Children's Photos: Allan Landau for ScottForesman

Page C6 David Young-Wolff/PhotoEdit **C8(ALL)** Courtesy Pittsburg Plate Glass Industries, Inc. **C9(ALL)** Courtesy Interstate Brick Co. **C10** Owen Franken/Stock Boston **C11** Milt & Joan Mann/Cameramann International, Ltd. **C15** Bruce Coleman, Inc. **C16** Wengle/DRK Photo **C17** Tom Ulrich/Visuals Unlimited **C18(T)** The Granger Collection, New York **C18(B)** Solomon D Butcher Collection/Nebraska State Historical Society **C19(L)** Philip E Harroun/Museum of New Mexico **C19(BR)** Jerry Jacka Photography **C22** Wendell Metzen **C27(L)** Don and Pat Valenti/f/stop **C27(R)** William J Weber/Visuals Unlimited **C30(L)** Culver Pictures **C30(R)** H. Armstrong Roberts **C31(L)** Milt & Joan Mann/ Cameramann International, Ltd. **C31(R)** Tony Freeman/Photo Edit **C34(L)** Courtesy Owens-Corning **C34(R)** Milt & Joan Mann/Cameramann International, Ltd. **C36(L)** Fred McConnaughey/Photo Researchers **C36(R)** Alex S. MacLean/Landslides **C37** Paolo Koch/Photo Researchers **C46-47(ALL)** Milt & Joan Mann/Cameramann International, Ltd. **C50(T)** John D. Cunningham/Visuals Unlimited **C50(B)** John D. Cunningham/Visuals Unlimited **C51(T)** B.J. Spenceley/Bruce Coleman, Inc. **C51(B)** S. Nielsen/DRK Photo **C52** Oxford Scientific Films/ANIMALS ANIMALS **C59(B)** Courtesy the FRANKLIN JOURNAL and The Farmington Maine Public Library **C60** Courtesy San Antonio Zoo

Illustrations
Page C3 Mas Miyamoto **C5** Blanche Sims **C6-7** Hank Iken **C17** Ebet Dudley **C26** Laurie O'Keefe **C30-31** Hank Iken **C32-33** Steve Fuller **C35** Peggy Tagel **C44-45** Mas Miyamoto **C56(T,B)** JAK Graphics **C61** Gary Torrisi

Module D
Photographs
Front & Back Cover: Background: Wayne Lankinen/DRK Photo   Children's Photos: Allan Landau for ScottForesman

Page D2(R) E.R.Degginger   **D3(T)** Culver Pictures **D3(B)** Joe McDonald/ANIMALS ANIMALS   **D5** Kerry T. Givens/Tom Stack & Associates   **D6** E.R.Degginger **D7** Maslowski/Visuals Unlimited   **D12(T)** Marty Snyderman/ Visuals Unlimited   **D12(B)** Jeff Foott/DRK Photo **D13(T)** Mary Clay/Tom Stack & Associates   **D13** Leonard Lee Rue III/ANIMALS ANIMALS   **D14(T)** Naval Photographic Center, Washington, D.C.   **D14(BL)** Dave B.Fleetham/ Tom Stack & Associates   **D14(BR)** Supplied by Carolina Biological Supply Company   **D15** Stephen Dalton/ANIMALS ANIMALS   **D18(T)** John D Cunningham/Visuals Unlimited **D18(B)** Maslowski Photo/Visuals Unlimited   **D18(C)** John D. Cunningham/Visuals Unlimited   **D21** Michael Fogden/ DRK Photo   **D22(T)** Peter Ward/Bruce Coleman, Inc. **D22(T INS)** Daniel Gotshall/Visuals Unlimited   **D22(B)** C.C. Lockwood/DRK Photo   **D22 (B INS)** Catherine Koehler **D23(T)** Science VU/Visuals Unlimited   **D23(T INS)** Alan & Sandy Carey   **D23B** Doug Allan/ANIMALS ANIMALS **D23(B INS)** Doug Wechsler/ANIMALS ANIMALS **D24** Wayne Lankinen/DRK Photo   **D25** E.R.Degginger **D28** P. Armstrong/Visuals Unlimited   **D29** Joe McDonald/ ANIMALS ANIMALS   **D30** Richard Ellis   **D31** Robert A Ross/E.R.Degginger   **D32(T)** Tom Edwards/Visuals Unlimited **D32B** Alan & Sandy Carey   **D36** Glenn Oliver/Visuals Unlimited   **D39** Culver Pictures   **D40(T)** INDIAN ENCAMPMENT ON LAKE HURON -Paul Kane 1845-50, Art Gallery of Ontario, Toronto   **D40(BL)** The Bettmann Archive **D40(BR)** Culver Pictures   **D41** Culver Pictures **D44(TL)** Culver Pictures   **D44(TR)** Culver Pictures **D44(CL)** The Bettmann Archive   **D44(CR)** The Bettmann Archive   **D44(BL)** Courtesy Ford Motor Company **D44(BR)** From the Collections of Henry Ford Museum & Greenfield Village   **D45(TL)** Culver Pictures   **D45(TR)** Milt & Joan Mann/Cameramann International, Ltd.   **D45(CR)** Courtesy Chrysler Corp.   **D45(BL)** Courtesy Kloster Cruise Ltd. **D45(BCL)** Douglas Aviation   **D45(BCR)** Brent Jones **D45(BR)** Courtesy Chrysler Corp.   **D45(CL)** Milt & Joan Mann/ Cameramann International, Ltd.   **D50** Mark W. Richards/Photo Edit   **D52** Takeshi Takahara/Photo Researchers   **D53** William Franklin McMahon/ScottForesman   **D58** David Young-Wolff/ Photo Edit   **D59** Robert Brenner/Photo Edit   **D60** Brent Jones/ Scott, Foresman

Illustrations
Page D2 Vincent Perez   **D6** Wild Onion Studio **D11** Vincent Perez   **D29, D30, D31, D32** JAK Graphics **D46-47** Pam Hohman   **D48-49** Ron Becker **D56** Simon Galkin   **D61** George Kelvin

Module E
Photographs
Front & Back Cover: Background: John Gerlach/DRK Photo Children's Photos: Allan Landau for ScottForesman

Page E5 Milt & Joan Mann/Cameramann International, Ltd. **E6** Milt & Joan Mann/Cameramann International, Ltd. **E7(T&B)** Milt & Joan Mann/Cameramann International, Ltd. **E11** Milt & Joan Mann/Cameramann International, Ltd. **E12(T)** Ben Goldstein/Don and Pat Valenti   **E12B** Alan & Sandy Carey   **E12(BR)** Kevin Doyle/Visuals Unlimited   **E19** John D. Cunningham/Visuals Unlimited   **E25** John Parnell/Telephoto

E27(T) Rod Planck/Tom Stack & Associates   **E27(B)** John Gerlach/DRK Photo   **E28** Stephen J Krasemann/DRK Photo **E29** Hans Pfletschinger/Peter Arnold, Inc.   **E34(T)** Bill Everitt/ Tom Stack & Associates   **E34 (T INS)** Bill Everitt/Tom Stack & Associates   **E34(B)** Arthur R. Hill/Visuals Unlimited **E34(B INS)** Arthur R. Hill/Visuals Unlimited **E35(T)** S. Maslowski/Visuals Unlimited **E35(T INS)** S. Maslowski/Visuals Unlimited   **E35(B)** Kjell B.Sandved/Visuals Unlimited   **E35(B INS)** Kjell B.Sandved/ Visuals Unlimited   **E36** Vaina Chen/Bruce Coleman, Inc. **E37(T)** Kjell B.Sandved/Visuals Unlimited   **E37(B)** Dennis Paulson/Visuals Unlimited   **E40** Rod Planck/Tom Stack & Associates   **E43** Bob Daemmrich   **E44** Tim Davis/Photo Researchers   **E48** Sybil Shelton/Peter Arnold, Inc.   **E49** Milt & Joan Mann/Cameramann International, Ltd.   **E50** Milt & Joan Mann/Cameramann International, Ltd.   **E51(TL)** AP/Wide World **E51(TC)** AP/Wide World   **E51(TR)** Milt & Joan Mann/ Cameramann International, Ltd.   **E51(BL)** ACME Photo/UPI/ Bettmann   **E51(BC)** Milt & Joan Mann/Cameramann International, Ltd.   **E51(BR)** Bob Daemmrich/Image Works **E52(T)** The Bettmann Archive   **E52(B)** The Bettmann Archive **E53** Laura Dwight   **E59** Myrleen Ferguson/Photo Edit **E60** Nathan Mandell/Scott, Foresman

Illustrations
Page E8-9 Ron Lipking   **E11-12** Susan Spellman **E18** Walter Stuart   **E22** Dale Glasgow   **E26** Catherine Twomey **E28** Laurie O'Keefe   **E29** Laurie O'Keefe   **E32-33** Catherine Twomey   **E50** JAK Graphics   **E56** JAK Graphics **E58-59** Carl Kock   **E61** Steve Fuller

Module F
Photographs
Front & Back Cover: Background: Marty Stouffer/ANIMALS ANIMALS   Children's Photos: Allan Landau for ScottForesman

Page F3(T) Clint Hansen   **F3(B)** William Peterson **F5** C.C.Lockwood/DRK Photo   **F8** E.R.Degginger **F13** Milt & Joan Mann/Cameramann International, Ltd. **F14** Bob Daemmrich   **F18** Don & Pat Valenti   **F22(T)** Brent Jones   **F22(B)** Tony Freeman/Photo Edit   **F23** Milt & Joan Mann/Cameramann International, Ltd.   **F39(ALL)** Milt & Joan Mann/Cameramann International, Ltd.   **F40** Link/Visuals Unlimited   **F42(L)** James Karales/Peter Arnold, Inc. **F42(R)** Bruce Berg/Visuals Unlimited   **F43(T)** Milt & Joan Mann/Cameramann International, Ltd.   **F43(B)** Tom Edwards/ Visuals Unlimited   **F44(T)** Tom McHugh/Photo Researchers **F44(B)** Marty Stouffer/ANIMALS ANIMALS   **F45(T)** Stephen J Krasemann/DRK Photo   **F45(B)** E.R.Degginger   **F46** Phil Degginger   **F47** John James Audubon, 1825/The New-York Historical Society, New York City   **F50** David Young-Wolff/Photo Edit   **F51(TL)** Dohra Lambrecht/Visuals Unlimited **F51(TC)** Peter Arnold, Inc.   **F51(TR)** Kerry T Givens/Tom Stack & Associates   **F51(B)** Dwight R. Kuhn   **F52** Wendell Metzen **F53** David R. Frazier Photolibrary   **F59** Fox5 TV/Kid City

Illustrations
Page F6-7 John Burgoyne   **F24** Hank Iken   **F32-33** Ron Becker   **F40-41** Clint Hansen   **F46** William Peterson **F47** JAK Graphics   **F61** Gary Torrisi